TACKLING TOUGH CHOICES

Discussion-Starting Skits for Teens

Doris Anita Anderson

Resource Publications, Inc.
San Jose, California

Also available in the ACTING IT OUT series:

Acting It Out: 74 Short Plays for Starting Discussions With Teenagers
 by Joan Sturkie and Marsh Cassady
Acting It Out Junior: Discussion Starters for 10-13 Year Olds
 by Marsh Cassady and Joan Sturkie
Facing Violence: Discussion-Starting Skits for Teenagers
 by R. William Pike
Facing Substance Abuse: Discussion-Starting Skits for Teenagers
 by R. William Pike

Reprint Department
Resource Publications, Inc.
160 E. Virginia Street #290
San Jose, CA 95112-5876
(408) 286-8505 voice
(408) 287-8748 fax

Library of Congress Cataloging-in-Publication Data
Anderson, Doris Anita, 1937–
 Tackling tough choices : discussion-starting skits for teens / Doris Anita Anderson.
  p.   cm. — (Acting it out series)
 ISBN 0-89390-518-6
 1. Teenagers—Conduct of life—Study and teaching. 2. Moral education (Secondary) 3. Drama in education. 4. Decision making in adolescence. I. Title. II. Series.

HQ796 .A6838 2001
305.235—dc21

2001041778

01 02 03 04 05 | 5 4 3 2 1

Editorial director: Nick Wagner
Editor: Kenneth Guentert
Production: Romina Saha
Copyeditor: Tricia Joerger
Cover design: Nelson Estarija

Contents

Being picked on

PART III: SEX VS. LOVE — CLEARING UP THE CONFUSION

Sending mixed signals

Being used

In the danger zone

Introduction

WATCHING teens making dangerous and life-changing choices can be very frustrating to caring adults who want them to grow up straight and strong. How to help them best can be perplexing. They want to do what they want to do. Often, it is only after they have suffered some kind of unwanted consequences that they see in perspective what has happened. How can adults help kids learn how to handle difficult situations in ways that are best for themselves and others?

"Pretend," or play-acting, has long been recognized as one way children learn social development. For teens, participating in realistic, problem-oriented dramas can help them safely and vicariously identify with the plays' fictional characters and their problems. They can discuss serious problems without exposing their own vulnerability. The students become engaged in their own learning, when in a structured and organized setting, they can identify, face, and choose the most appropriate solutions to complex problems the characters may face. Often, there is no nice, clean solution. But there is always a best solution even if mistakes have already been made or if the teens are in a mess through no fault of their own.

The plays in this book are based on real events in real teens' lives. The situations are not written to place blame on others, thereby removing responsibility from the teens for their circumstances. They are written to help teens face situations as they are, to try to understand why others behave the way they do, and then to take responsibility for their own actions. The questions at the end of each drama are written in a way to lead the students toward an ethical, logical, and appropriate solution.

A deep-seated need of kids (and of all of us) is to be "cool," to handle things well. Having a well-developed and rational thought process to use in times of trouble gives a sense of self-confidence and well-being. Not only can developing this ability help diffuse potential conflicts around a school or neighborhood, but it can make happier, better adjusted students, who in turn, will be better able to learn.

I deliberately chose not to use actual profanity in these skits although some swear words might seem more natural and powerful. I didn't want the language to call attention to itself, be a cause for giggling, or justify the use of profanity in a school setting. The stories should be effective without it.

The following tips may help make these skits more effective:

- During the discussion, be sure all students get a chance to respond to the questions. The very quiet or shy ones often have thoughtful and knowledgeable comments.
- Be sure that all students' responses are listened to respectfully. Insist that there be no derogatory comments or name-calling.
- Encourage students to be honest in responding to the various ways the characters can handle their problems. Doing nothing is always an option, but it usually doesn't solve anything. Students may suggest violent retaliation on an enemy. This and most other ideas should be permissible for discussion, for it lets students express their frustration honestly. However, ample and effective discussion should lead to safe, logical, and appropriate resolutions that don't hurt the victim and don't further enable the perpetrators to continue their bad behavior.

- This book is designed to be used on an impromptu basis—without props or preparation—in a classroom and small-group setting. Detailed stage directions are included to help readers better imagine the characters, their personalities, and their actions. When reading the scenes aloud, assign someone the job of reading all the stage directions. Reading the stage directions aloud will help the group to grasp the dynamics of the scene and to better understand the information it conveys.
- It may be helpful to have students take a few minutes to write responses to the questions in a journal so that they can reflect for a while before beginning the class discussion.
- An important part of the learning in these dramas centers on how to get help for difficult problems. It would be useful to have on hand an up-to-date directory of school and community resources that can provide support groups, counseling, legal assistance, financial aid, and so forth.

May all who use this book with teens know the rush of satisfaction that comes from seeing them engaged in their own learning, especially as it builds good character and teaches useful coping skills. Discussion-starting dramas can be a powerful tool to help kids learn to think through and productively solve some of the dilemmas modern kids face.

PART I: PROBLEMS WITH PARENTS

How much
should they be involved?

Mom Lives in the Dark Ages

CHARACTERS

BONNIE, CARLOS, NITA, MOM, DAD (divorced from mom)

School has just let out. CARLOS and NITA want BONNIE to go with them to the mall. MOM will be home from work at four-thirty and expects BONNIE to come straight home, do her homework, and start supper. BONNIE has been in trouble for ditching school.

CARLOS   Well, girl, are you on? Remember, today's the day.

BONNIE   Oh, yeah. I remember. The mall, right?

NITA   Aren't you still on restriction? I thought you said after you got busted for ditching that your mom sentenced you for two weeks.

BONNIE   Oh, yeah. It's been a week. That's enough. My mom overreacts big time.

CARLOS   Yeah, my mom's like that too. They forget what it's like to be young. So you're coming?

BONNIE   Sure. I'm on. Let's go. I'll think of something to tell her.

NITA   You sure?

BONNIE   Yeah, especially if you'll let me copy your homework for Collins' class. I'm three chapters behind. It's so boring.

CARLOS   Hey, I can give it to you. I already copied it from Nita. It's in the trunk of my car.

Later, in the mall, the three are in a music store looking at CDs.

NITA   Hey, girl, you got this one? He's so cool. I can't play it when my dad's around, though. He says the words are trash. So I play it in my room.

BONNIE   Yeah, I've got that one. Shoot, I know most of the words by heart. You know, "I need your body." (*They laugh with each other, then begin moving to the beat of the music on the store speakers.*) Can you believe my mom thinks she can control what I listen to?

CARLOS   Hey, I heard a guy say that modern music speaks the energy of the young. The old folks always criticize the new stuff.

NITA   And make-up and clothes. Hey, the young set the trends. I saw this grandma-looking woman wearing a tube top the other day. I think it was so she could show her tattoos. But she was a little too old to look good, know what I mean? (*She screws her face up into a disgusted grimace. The other two laugh derisively.*)

CARLOS   Gross.

BONNIE   You know, I've been thinking of getting a tattoo. Right here. (*She points to the back of her shoulder.*) What do you guys think?

NITA   Cool. What kind of a design do you want? I know a guy in third period who draws custom designs for kids. I think he charges ten dollars. He makes anything you want.

CARLOS   Well, girl, you're only sixteen, aren't you? You can't get one at a regular parlor. Unless your mom signs that she gives you her permission.

BONNIE   Naw, she'd never do that. She lives in the dark ages.

CARLOS   But she does keep a roof over your head and food on the table, doesn't she?

BONNIE   (*ignoring his last remarks*)   But your uncle, he does tattoos out of his house, doesn't he? I've got forty dollars saved up. You think he could do a nice butterfly for me?

The clerk moves over near the kids and asks them if they need any help. They drift out of the store.

BONNIE Man, that clerk is pushy. But she doesn't know what I got in my jacket. (*She opens her jacket pocket for the other two to look in. Inside is a CD she has just stolen.*)

NITA Whoa. Wow! You're really sly, girl. Hey, I don't want to get caught. They'd haul us all in a back room, call the cops, then call our mothers. Been there, done that. No more.

BONNIE Well, I'm too clever for that. Since my mom has been keeping my allowance for herself, I have to take care of my own needs. Know what I mean?

CARLOS (*feeling a little uneasy*) Uh-oh. What time is it? I gotta get home by six or I'll miss dinner. (*They begin heading for his parked car.*)

BONNIE Your mom won't save dinner for you if you're not home on time? Hey, that's not fair.

CARLOS Try to tell her that. That's the one rule she's tough on. The rest of the time I can sweet-talk her into almost anything.

BONNIE Well, you're lucky. My mom expects me to start dinner when she has to work late. That sucks. She could pick up something on the way home.

NITA Well, hey, this conversation is a dud. How about you guys coming over to my place Saturday night? We can party a little and lighten things up. My folks are going to Vegas.

CARLOS Sounds good. What do you think, Bonnie? Think your mom will let you off restriction by then? I could pick you up.

BONNIE Well yeah, I gotta be there. My mom doesn't own my life. I'll find a way. Maybe I can claim I have a headache, go to bed early, then I'll sneak out the window and call you from the phone booth down the street.

MOM comes home about six-thirty. No dinner is started, and BONNIE is in her room listening to the CD she stole.

MOM (*calling*) Bonnie? Bonnie? (*She opens BONNIE's door and is hit with a loud blast of music.*) Bonnie! Shut that thing off.

BONNIE What?

MOM (*louder*) Shut that thing off!

BONNIE (*Angrily reaches over and shuts off the music.*) What's up, Mom? (*seeing MOM's frown*) I was just listening to this new CD Carlos let me borrow.

MOM I told you to stick the meatloaf in the oven by five. It should be ready now.

BONNIE Oh, that's right. I forgot. But you know how I hate getting my hands all greasy mixing that stuff up.

MOM (*Her shoulders drop in disappointment.*) Bonnie, I need to be able to count on you to help me out. I've worked hard all day, and I'm tired and hungry. Now we won't be able to eat until about eight. What have you been doing anyway? Did you at least get your homework done?

BONNIE Oh, that's all taken care of. Carlos is helping me with it.

Friday afternoon, MOM has come home early from work. There is a message on the answering machine that BONNIE was absent the last two periods on Thursday. The school wants the mother to come in for a conference about BONNIE's truancies. BONNIE should have been home by four, but she comes straggling in at five-thirty. Her hair is tousled. She is wearing the low-cut t-shirt her mother has forbidden her to wear to school.

MOM (*angrily*) Where have you been?

BONNIE You're home early?

MOM Answer the question.

BONNIE Carlos gave me a ride home, but he had to run a couple of errands on the way. Sorry.

MOM   Sorry is right. It's five-thirty. It took you an hour and a half to run a couple of errands? And why is your hair all messed up?

BONNIE (*getting snotty*)   Mom, I've got a right to my own life. You don't need to be in my face all the time. Besides, it's none of your business where I was. I have a right to my own life. Stay out of my face.

MOM   You're telling *me* to stay out of your face? Well, you ain't seen nothin' yet, child. I just got a message from the school that you've been ditching again. And now, I've got to take time off work to go in for a conference.

BONNIE   So what? School sucks, too.

MOM   Great attitude, Bonnie. I guess you think you can live for free the rest of your life. You're not going to be able to get any kind of decent job without an education.

BONNIE (*holding up her hand*)   Talk to this, Mom. I've heard that so many times … I'm still a kid. I thought adults were into wanting kids to stay kids for a while instead of growing up so fast.

MOM   Forget that! You're in big trouble now. From now on, no more rides home with Carlos. You walk. And you *will* start dinner. And you *will* clean up that dump of a room. And now you're on restriction for a month.

BONNIE (*angrily*)   Screw you, Mom. You can't tell me what to do! I've got rights! (*She gets up and stalks out to the kitchen, picks up the phone.*) Dad, it's me, your Baby Girl.

DAD (*His voice is heard on the phone.*)   Oh, hi, Bonnie. You kinda caught me at a bad time. Can I call you back? We're in the middle of a birthday party for—

BONNIE   Dad, Dad, wait a minute. I need you to listen. I gotta get outta here. Mom is in my face all the time.

DAD   Bonnie, I can't really talk right now. Quick. What is it?

BONNIE   Dad, can you send me some money so I can come and stay there? The school's on my back, too. I can't stand it. Please?

DAD   Honey, this is just a temporary phase. It'll pass. Just be cool. (*pause*) Honey, you know I'd love to have you here, but you know there's no more room. The new baby took up the spare bedroom for a nursery. Just try to work things out, will you? I'll call you back when I get a minute. (*He hangs up.*)

Discussion

1. Is Bonnie's mother being unreasonable by putting her on restriction for ditching and asking her to start dinner?
2. Why do you think Bonnie is such a problem to her mother? Is her dad being fair to her?
3. Can you think of other ways that Bonnie's mother could deal with her daughter's bad behavior?
4. How do you think the mother feels about how her daughter is acting?
5. If Bonnie keeps up her rebellious behavior and stealing, what is likely to happen?
6. If you were a counselor, what would you recommend that might help Bonnie?

Mom Snoops in My Room When I'm Gone

CHARACTERS
BERT, MARILYN, MOM, BRIANNA, DONNIE

BERT, MARILYN and BRIANNA are eating lunch in the cafeteria.

BRIANNA   So, Marilyn, I hear you and Donnie are getting kinda close, know what I mean?

MARILYN   Where'd you hear that? (*Giggles slyly.*) Actually, he really treats me nice. He's not like any other guy I've ever hung around with. But my mom doesn't like him hanging around so much.

BRIANNA   Why is that?

MARILYN (*shrugs*)   Heck, I don't know how my mom thinks. But she's way too nosy about my business.

BRIANNA   Well, at least she pays attention to you.

MARILYN   Yeah, I guess. But I think I'd rather live with my dad. When I go there in the summers, he treats me like a grown up. You know, no curfews, lets me go out with anybody I want.

BRIANNA   Really? Well, I do think your mom is nice. But she is kinda strict. You think she'll let you go to the movies with me and Bert Saturday night? We don't need to tell her that Donnie is coming along.

MARILYN   Hey, that sounds like a plan. What she doesn't know won't hurt her.

BRIANNA   Yeah. Tell her I'm driving. I'll pick you up first, then we'll go get Bert and Donnie. If she doesn't see any guys in the car, she probably won't care if you come in late.

BERT (*approaching table*)   Hey, Marilyn. What's up? You and Donnie going to be able to come Saturday night?

MARILYN   Well, we gotta fool my mom. After she smelled liquor on my breath and found out I wasn't really studying at the library till ten o'clock last time, she told me Donnie was a bad influence and she didn't want me going out with him.

BERT   Well, we can get around that. Donnie thinks you're hot, you know. And he can get any girl he wants.

MARILYN (*blushing*)   Yeah, I know.

In MARILYN's house later that day, MOM is fixing dinner. MARILYN is in her room sitting on her bed and writing in her diary.

MARILYN (*Her voice reads the words she has written.*)   "So, it should be fun Saturday night with Brianna and Bert. Donnie probably won't want to drink with them around. I hope. I wish I didn't like him so much. It kinda scares me. He's done so much. I don't want him to think I'm a baby. My mom would croak if she knew I'd been over to his place when his folks were gone. He really turns me on." (*MOM pops in the door. MARILYN quickly hides her diary under her pillow.*)

MOM   Dinner's ready, honey. You get your homework all done?

MARILYN   Almost, Mom. I'll be right there.

MOM   Okay. (*She looks around at the messy room.*) Honey, when you get a minute, you've got to clean up this mess.

MARILYN   Yeah, Mom. I will. Uh, by the way, would you care if I go to a movie with Brianna Saturday night?

MOM   Oh, I guess not, if you get this room cleaned up.

MARILYN   I will, Mom. I promise.

After the movie, BRIANNA and BERT have dropped DONNIE and MARILYN off at DONNIE's house. His parents are out of town but have left him their car so he can give MARILYN a ride home. DONNIE has poured himself a drink of bourbon and is offering MARILYN one.

DONNIE   Come on, baby. You've gotta loosen up. (*He hands her the glass.*)

MARILYN (*Hesitates, then takes the glass.*)   Well, I guess I could taste it. The wine last time was sweet, but I don't know about whiskey. (*Takes a sip.*) Oooh. It kinda burns. (*Sets the glass down on the coffee table.*)

DONNIE (*Puts on some romantic music, then sits down close beside her.*)   Is that all you're going to drink, baby? Come on, it'll make you feel good. And we're finally alone. I've been wanting to show you how much I like you. (*Hands her the glass from the coffee table.*) Here, drink up. You're still so tense.

MARILYN (*Feels a little uneasy, but takes several swallows.*)   I don't get why you like this stuff. It's so strong. How long have you been drinking, anyway?

DONNIE (*pulling her close*)   Oh, since I was about nine. Gosh, you smell good. (*They listen to the music a few minutes. DONNIE begins to kiss her, then pushes her down on the couch.*)

MARILYN (*nervously*)   Easy, Donnie. (*beginning to feel a little high*)

DONNIE   Come on, baby. Just relax. I won't hurt you.

MARILYN's mom is asleep when she sneaks in. The next Monday, while MARILYN is in school, MOM goes into her room to hang up a coat. The room is still messy, so she begins to pick up clothes and carry them to the hamper. Then she begins to make the bed. Under the pillow, she finds MARILYN's diary.

MOM (*reading from diary*)   "So I got kinda drunk for the first time. My head was spinning around. And I told Donnie not to be in such a hurry, but I don't want to be uncool. I mean, everybody's gotta start sometime. And he really knows how to turn me on. . ." (*MOM looks up and shakes her head.*) My little girl's been sneaking around on me.

After school that day, MOM is waiting for MARILYN when she comes in.

MOM   So, do you want to tell me the truth about Saturday night?

MARILYN   What? You know I just went to the movie with Brianna. She did meet her boyfriend Bert there. (*pause*) What's the matter? You think I'm lying? (*sarcastically*) Boy, that makes me feel good.

MOM   I need you to tell me the truth, Marilyn.

MARILYN   I did tell you the truth, Mom.

MOM   Marilyn, I know better. You were drinking and you were with that Donnie.

MARILYN   Mom, what makes you think that? I can't stand it when you accuse me. I'm not a baby, you know. (*She stalks into her room and slams the door.*)

MOM (*following her*)   Don't lie to me, Marilyn.

MARILYN (*Sees her room tidied up and her bed made. The diary is lying on top of the pillow.*)   Oh, my gosh. You read my diary, Mom. How dare you! How dare you? You have no right to snoop into my business!

MOM   And just whose house do you think this is anyway?

Discussion

1. Does Marilyn deserve to be trusted? Explain.
2. Does Marilyn deserve absolute privacy in her room? Why or why not?
3. What are Mom's concerns for her daughter?
4. Was Mom wrong for reading Marilyn's diary? Explain.
5. Name all the ways Marilyn could handle this situation, both bad and good.
6. If you were Marilyn's mom, what would you do?

Fathers — How Important Are They?

CHARACTERS

LORI, SAM, ROBERT, ANGELA, MRS. CARLYLE (teacher)

In life skills class, students are seated in a circle. MRS. CARLYLE is leading a discussion of parenting.

MRS. CARLYLE So, students, I'd like you to reflect on how you feel about the role of fathers in your own lives. Today we know some people live together without benefit of marriage, have children together, and they seem to feel that's okay for the kids. If the relationship doesn't work out, one or the other will move out, and some think that's okay too. Then casual sex is so common. And we know babies happen. So I'd like you to reflect on how this carefree attitude affects those little babies, especially the importance of the babies' fathers. Think about your own situations. Then, if you're willing to share, we'll go around the circle, and you can express how your own father has influenced your life. Does anyone want to start? (*SAM raises his hand.*) Okay, Sam.

SAM Well, for me, the dude only shows up about once a year. That's okay, because he wants to be all buddy-buddy, but I don't know him that well. Heck, it's my grandpa who takes me fishing and helps my mom watch out for me.

ANGELA So you feel you don't need your father then?

SAM Not really. The dude's never done nothing for me. My mom works her butt off and he never sent any child support.

ANGELA Is that why you call him "dude"? That seems kinda, you know, old-fashioned.

SAM Yeah, I guess so. I think he thinks he's still living in the time of peace and love. You know, if it feels good, it's okay.

MRS. CARLYLE So, Sam, are you maybe a little bitter?

SAM (*He is quiet a moment.*) Well, I sure will be there for my own kids. Yeah, I guess it makes me feel that I'm not very valuable to him.

MRS. CARLYLE Thanks, Sam. Who'd like to go next?

ANGELA I will. Well, I totally adore my dad. He's funny. He loves my mom. He works so hard for us. (*She looks around the group at the thoughtful faces.*) I guess I'm really lucky. Any boyfriend I have, I measure them up to my dad.

MRS. CARLYLE Wow! That's really nice. Have you told him how much you love and respect and appreciate him?

ANGELA I think he knows.

ROBERT Man, I'm kinda sad, now. My dad died when I was five. He used to look at me with those eyes, and I knew he was so proud I was his son. I tried to let him know how much I loved him … (*He pauses to regain his composure. He looks at ANGELA.*) Tell him every chance you get how much you love him.

MRS. CARLYLE Thanks, Robert. You're so right. Parents need to know their kids love them and appreciate what they do for them, too. But today, as we think about our parents, especially our fathers, it means so much to us to know they love us unconditionally. And what do you think "unconditionally" means? Lori, you haven't said anything yet.

LORI Uh, okay. I'll try. (*She is dressed in torn Levi shorts. Her blouse is cut so low that her bra shows.*) I think it means that … you'll do anything for someone you love, anytime. (*Lori giggles and shuffles her feet.*)

ANGELA   What kinda love are you talking about, girl? I think Mrs. Carlyle means how should parents love their kids. Isn't that what you meant, Mrs. Carlyle?

MRS. CARLYLE   Yes, I did. You all know there are different kinds of love we have for others, and parental love is like no other. Can you tell us, Lori, how you think parents should love their kids, especially, since today's focus is on fathers, what role fathers should play in loving their kids?

LORI   Okay. I gotta think about this a little. You see, I live with my grandma. I don't think I've ever met my dad. Mom hasn't been able to tell me much about him. She has trouble keeping her own life together. And she's gone a lot. So, I guess, if you're talking stereotypes …

SAM   There she goes with those big words again. (*They all laugh.*)

LORI   Well, I guess dads are supposed to go to work and buy things for their family. They probably should actually marry the mother. They should take the family on vacations. (*She pauses.*) How's that?

ROBERT   Okay. But you talked mostly about money, you know, dads as provider. Where does the unconditional love come in?

LORI   (*LORI looks at him a moment. Her face goes sad.*)   Well, I think it means he never hits or calls names. (*She pauses and looks around the group.*) Wow, I guess I don't understand what you mean when you talk about unconditional love.

MRS. CARLYLE   I hope you don't mind, kids, but I'd like to chime in here. I'll share something that psychologists all know. A child's sense of self-worth begins by how they are treated by their parents. You kids know this in your hearts even if you've never said it in words before. From a good mother, a child learns nurturing and safety and that there is someone there to comfort them. From a good father, a child learns also about being protected, how to handle troubles. A boy learns from his dad how to treat women, and how to love his own wife when the time comes. A little boy learns patience, and kindness, and the importance of respecting himself and others. And a little girl learns how good men are supposed to treat women. She learns that she is precious and then she feels good about herself. What do you kids think about what I've said?

SAM   Sounds good, but I don't see that happening much. I see a lot of messed up people out there.

ANGELA   Yeah, me too. I guess I'm really lucky.

ROBERT   Well, that's the kind of dad I want to be. I hope I can find a girl who wants that too.

LORI   I've never found any guys like that. If I did, they probably wouldn't want me. Besides, I don't want some guy thinking I'm going to wear my little apron and be miss kissy housewife and make him look like the king.

MRS. CARLYLE   Well, I can see we need to discuss this a little more. Think about what we've said here today. Take a little time now and write your reflections of today's conversation in your journals. But first, I'm going to pass out these emergency cards for you to fill out. The office has to have them on file in case we have to call someone if you get sick or hurt at school. (*She rises and begins to pass out the cards.*) Fill them out completely, please. Thanks. (*The kids fill out their emergency cards and begin writing in their journals.*)

At her desk after class, MRS. CARLYLE is separating the cards and journals. She pauses and reads part of Lori's card aloud.

MRS. CARLYLE   Oh, my goodness. She wrote, "Father — unknown."

MRS. CARLYLE opens LORI's journal.

MRS. CARLYLE   I wonder what she wrote about today's discussion. (*She begins to read aloud.*) "Today's discussion sucked."

LORI (*LORI's voice continues from what is written in her journal.*)   Angela makes me sick. That's mean of me to say, I guess, because I think she likes to brag all the time. She's got the latest clothes. Shoot, I guess maybe I'm a little bit jealous. But I'll have my boyfriend waiting to pick me up after school. He's better than nothing, I guess. He does have a car, even if he does get a little rough sometimes." (*MRS. CARLYLE puts the journal down, shakes her head sadly, and stares out the window.*)

Discussion

1. Why do you think the teacher, Mrs. Carlyle, wanted her students to reflect on the importance of fathers in their lives? How do kids learn what a good father is?
2. What is Sam's conflict concerning his father? If his father can't make time for Sam in his life, how else might Sam search for a sense of self-worth?
3. What kind of a father do you think Sam will be to his own children?
4. Because his father died when Robert was a child, what conflicts do you think he is likely to face as he grows up? What kind of father do you think Robert will be to his own children?
5. Lori doesn't know her father at all or even who he is. How do you think this affects her sense of self-worth as a young woman?
6. What could help Lori understand how a father should love his child? What could help her choose a good father for her own children?
7. What are the most important qualities a good father should have to help his children grow up strong, happy, kind, and confident?

Mom Likes My Friends Too Much

CHARACTERS
JESSICA, BARRY, MISTI, HENRY, MOM

The four teens are sitting around an outdoor school lunch table.

BARRY   So, do you guys wanna come over tonight and watch some videos? I think my mom'll be at work.

MISTI   Sounds cool. What do you think, Henry?

HENRY   Well, I've got some studying to do, but I can hang around a while.

MISTI (*to BARRY*)   Your mom's really easy going, isn't she? Gosh, my mom gets all upset if I want friends over very often. She thinks the house is never clean enough. I think she's trying to tell me something. (*giggles*)

JESSICA (*giving BARRY a little hug*)   Yeah. His mom likes to see us having a good time. She even wants to hang out with us sometimes. My mom would never do that.

BARRY (*He shrugs.*)   Yeah. She does. Well, I'll see you guys about seven then, okay?

HENRY   Yeah, okay then.

The four are lounging around in BARRY's living room discussing what video to watch.

JESSICA   Honestly, you guys always want to watch the stuff with blood and guts.

BARRY   Well, that's because we're so manly. You gotta appreciate us for who we are. Right? (*They all laugh.*)

MISTI   Oh, sure. But I'd like to watch this new music video.

HENRY   Hey, if you want someone to shake their stuff. (*He gets up and twitches his hips.*)

MOM enters. She is wearing a skin-tight stretch top and tights. She raises her arms above her head and begins to dance directly in front of HENRY. BARRY turns a little red.

MOM (*MOM stops suddenly when she notices the kids staring at her. She speaks in a syrupy voice.*)   Hi. What are you kids doing? (*MOM looks at MISTI holding the video.*) Oh, hey, put that on. I just love that group.

BARRY   Mom, I thought you'd still be at work.

MOM (*She stands still and stares at him.*)   No. I worked the early shift today. Why?

BARRY   Uh, Mom, we were going to watch this war movie. You wouldn't like it, I don't think.

The kids watch silently.

MOM   Oh, I get it. (*She twirls her hips a couple of times, looking at HENRY.*) I was hoping we could all dance a little. You know, get it on. Isn't that what you kids say these days? I need some exercise.

BARRY   Mom, that's not what we were gonna do. Sorry.

JESSICA (*giving BARRY a knowing look*)   Uh, oh gosh, look at the time. I forgot I gotta finish my book report tonight. I better go. (*She grabs her jacket and heads for the door.*)

MOM   Oh, I'm sorry. Being in school is tough. I forgot. I don't have to be to work tomorrow till noon. But the rest of us can watch the movie if you guys want.

MISTI   Thanks anyway, but I gotta go too. I was only going to stay a little while anyway. (*She starts for the door.*) Well, see you guys in school tomorrow. Bye.

HENRY   Wait up. I'll walk you home. See ya, Barry. (*He turns to Barry's MOM.*) Bye. Nice to see you again. (*exits*)

MOM   Well, what's wrong with them? I thought you were going to watch the movie.

BARRY   Mom, we thought you'd be working late. We didn't want to bother you.

MOM (*pause*)   You mean, you don't want me bothering you. I get it. Now that you're a big teen macho jock, you can't stand to have your little old mom around anymore. I get it.

BARRY   Mom, that's not it. It's just that … teens need to hang out with teens and grownups need to hang out with grownups.

MOM   So you're saying that you don't want me around anymore when you have your friends over, is that it? You don't want your mom around who provides a roof over your head, food on the table, clothes on your back. Listen, my dad would've knocked me across the room if I'd acted this way toward him. What happened to kids respecting their parents?

Discussion

1. Why do you think Barry's mom wants to be with him and his friends?
2. Is her behavior appropriate? Explain.
3. Why do you think Barry and his friends don't want her around when they're hanging out?
4. What choices does Barry have for how to handle this situation? You should come up with at least three.
5. For each choice, who would be helped or hurt?
6. If you were in Barry's situation, what would you do?

When things really aren't right

Dad Doesn't Care What I Do

CHARACTERS
 HARVEY, DAD, CONRAD, MARJORIE, ANGIE

HARVEY and DAD are in the living room watching television. The phone rings.

DAD   You've got "The Den." What's up? Or should I say what's on? (*pause*) Oh, hi, Weasel. Yeah, I got some. But you owe me big time.

HARVEY (*talking to himself*)   I hate that guy.

DAD (*still on the phone, ignoring HARVEY*)   Hey, man, that's your problem. I don't do business for nothing. (*pause*) Well, maybe. What you got? (*pause*) Yeah, I could use that. Where are you right now? (*pause*) Okay. I'll be right over. I'll bring my truck. You'll have it in the garage, right? (*pause*) Yeah, yeah. I'll bring you some. (*He hangs up, turns and looks at HARVEY as he rises and heads for the door.*) Hey, Harve, be cool, huh? I'll be back in a while. (*exits*)

HARVEY (*Flips channels a few minutes, to himself.*)   Man. This is boring. I won't see him till tomorrow. Shoot. I wonder what Conrad's doing. (*He dials a number.*) Hey, Conrad.

CONRAD (*His voice is heard on phone.*)   Harve, man, what's up?

HARVEY   Hey, man, ya doing anything? I got the place to myself. Come on over. There's stuff in the refrigerator, if you get my drift. We can kick back and relax.

CONRAD   Your dad's gone again? (*pause*) Yeah. I'd like to kick back. Listen, Marjorie's here. Care if she comes, too? She's cool.

HARVEY   Hey, no, man. Come on over, both of you. I got enough for the three of us. She got any friends? Tell her to bring her too. Okay, then. See ya soon. (*He hangs up phone.*)

In a few minutes, there is a knock at the door.

HARVEY (*rising and opening the door*)   Hey, cool. (*to CONRAD*) And who is this hot babe? (*He motions to ANGIE.*)

CONRAD   Harve, my friend, meet Angie. She lives next door to Marjorie.

HARVEY   Well, come on in. (*The three guests crowd into the small living room.*) Hey, make yourselves comfortable. You guys want something to drink? Dad always keeps lots of beer in the refrigerator.

MARJORIE   Cool. Yeah, Angie and I are drying up.

ANGIE   Uh, yeah, okay, I guess.

CONRAD   Oh, it's okay, Angie. His dad doesn't care.

HARVEY (*under his breath*)   That's right, he doesn't care. (*to the rest*) Okay, you guys. Put on a video. There's a stack over there on the shelf. I'll be right back. (*He exits to kitchen.*)

MARJORIE   What do you guys want to watch? (*She looks at several videos.*) Uh-oh. Here's a naughty one. (*She giggles; to HARVEY as he comes back into the room carrying four beers*) Your dad lets you watch this stuff? (*She turns it over and looks at the cover.*) Wow! This looks like a porno. You watch this stuff?

ANGIE (*to herself*)   Gosh, what did I get myself into?

HARVEY   Those're my dad's. He doesn't care what I watch.

CONRAD (*to the girls*)   Hey, we don't need to watch that one. Isn't there a *Mary Poppins* over there, or something? (*They all laugh.*)

MARJORIE   Conrad! We're not babies.

CONRAD   You look more like babes to me. (*They all laugh again.*)

ANGIE   Harvey, when's your dad coming home?

HARVEY   Probably not for a while. When he takes off in his truck in the evening, I usually don't see him till the next day.

ANGIE   Does he do that a lot?

HARVEY   Yeah, I guess so. That's why Mom left.

MARJORIE   Gosh, I didn't know that. How long's your mom been gone? I bet you miss her, huh?

CONRAD   The party's getting too serious. Hey, maybe Harvey'd rather not talk about it. And so, I propose a toast to Harve, for inviting us over. To Harvey ... (*They clink bottles, laugh a little.*)

MARJORIE (*She sits back down.*)   Well, you guys pick a video. But not a real dirty one, please.

HARVEY   Okay. I'll put on one that's PG rated. (*under his breath*) I hate it when Dad watches these things all the time. (*to the others as he slides in a video*) But drink up, we got lots of beer.

CONRAD (*to HARVEY*)   Hey, Harve, he didn't leave you any of that good weed, did he? Man, that last stuff was the best.

HARVEY   Yeah, he always leaves me some. He says it'll keep me company when he's gone doing business at night. (*pause*) I can share. (*pause, to Conrad*) You sure Angie's down for this? She doesn't act like she's been around too much.

CONRAD   Yeah, man, she's down. That's why she's here. Besides, you're cool to be around, man. Let the party really begin.

Discussion

1. What kind of a father is Harvey's dad?
2. Is he being good to Harvey by letting him drink and smoke pot?
3. Do you think Conrad, Marjorie, and Angie really value Harvey as a true friend?
4. Do you think Harvey feels good about all the freedom his dad gives him? Explain.
5. Do you think Harvey respects his dad? Explain.
6. Harvey has several ways he can handle this situation, both bad and good. Name them.
7. If you were Harvey's counselor, how would you try to help him?
8. If you were in a similar situation, what would you do?

Can I Just Put My Head Down Today?

CHARACTERS

KEVIN, MARSHA, BOBBY, LaVONNE, MR. JAMISON

Students are congregated in the hall outside the door of MR. JAMISON's first period science class. He overhears their conversation.

MARSHA Man, Kevin, you look like you were dragged behind a truck last night. Are you okay?

KEVIN Huh? Sorry. I'm a little out of it today.

MARSHA That's what I noticed. Are you okay?

KEVIN Yeah. I'll be okay after this coffee kicks in. Maybe about eleven o'clock. (*He gives a wry little smile.*)

BOBBY Hey, I think he's hung over. Come on, you can tell us. We'll keep our mouths shut.

LaVONNE Yeah, Kevin. Been there, done that! (*She laughs, but the others just look at her.*)

KEVIN Well, I think I'll have to keep my mouth shut. My mom couldn't get in trouble, could she? I mean, I'm a big boy. I can think for myself.

BOBBY (*incredulously*) Are you saying you drank with your mother? Wow. I wish my mom was so cool.

LaVONNE Yeah. Mine would kill me if she knew some of the sneaky ways I get my alcohol. She hates booze, but she forgot what it's like to be young.

KEVIN But I didn't really want to drink last night. Man, I'll never graduate if I can't get my homework done. (*He pauses.*) She was lonesome, I guess. Her boyfriend moved out on her.

MARSHA I guess you don't live with your mom, huh?

KEVIN No, not anymore. I've been staying at my uncle's house, just till I graduate, he says.

The bell rings. The kids move into the classroom and sit down. Kevin puts his head down.

MR. JAMISON (*He moves over beside KEVIN, sits down in an empty chair next to him, and tries to look into his face.*) Excuse me. Kevin? Are you going to be okay? Did you party last night?

KEVIN (*KEVIN raises his head and looks into MR. JAMISON's concerned face.*) Uh, I guess you could say that.

MR. JAMISON Did you get any sleep at all?

KEVIN Not much. I'll just say that I fell asleep on the couch after we finished the vodka.

MR. JAMISON How old are you now, Kevin? Seventeen, sixteen?

KEVIN I just turned seventeen. But I've been drinking for a long time. I'm a big boy. I can handle this. I'll be okay. Thanks for asking. But can I just keep my head down in class today? I promise I'll have the work done for you tomorrow.

MR. JAMISON Well, there's nothing either of us can do about this right now. At least you're here. But I *am* concerned about this.

BOBBY (*He has been watching the conversation.*) He's cool, Mr. Jamison.

LaVONNE (*trying to direct attention away from KEVIN*) Uh, Mr. Jamison. You're not going to believe this, but I've got my homework done. You want me to pick up everybody's papers for you?

MR. JAMISON Sure. Thanks, LaVonne. (*She gets up and begins to collect homework papers. KEVIN puts his head back down.*)

Discussion

1. What is Kevin's main problem in this story?
2. Do you think Kevin's mom loves him? Does he love her?
3. Does getting drunk with her help or hurt their relationship?
4. What is Kevin's mother's conflict? How can Kevin best help his mother?
5. Why do you think Bobby and LaVonne tried to smooth things over for Kevin?
6. Name ways Mr. Jamison might be able to help Kevin deal with his mother and the drinking.
7. If Kevin does nothing about this situation, what is likely to happen in the future?
8. If you were the school counselor and you learned about Kevin's situation, what would you do?

Dad's Been Drinking Again

CHARACTERS

DAD, MOM, GINA and TONY (brother and sister), ANDREA (a neighborhood friend)

GINA, TONY, and ANDREA are walking home from school.

ANDREA   So, Gina, are you gonna be at the football game tonight? I know someone who's going to be there who'd kinda like to, you know, get acquainted.

TONY   Yeah, Gin-Gin. You know you need to get out a little more. All that holing up in your room is getting on my nerves.

GINA   You guys. (*She blushes.*) And Tony, I asked you not to call me Gin-Gin. You know why. (*She turns to ANDREA.*) I would like to know who wants to get acquainted, but tell me when my nosy brother isn't around.

ANDREA   But first you've gotta come to the game. Will you?

GINA   I don't know. It depends on how things are at home. I'd like to come, but sometimes Mom needs me.

TONY   Aw, Gina. Mom's grown up. You don't need to take care of her.

ANDREA   Is your mom sick or something?

GINA   Well, not exactly, but …

ANDREA   Hey, I don't mean to be in your business …

GINA   It's okay. (*They have come to GINA and TONY's house.*) Well, I'll see you at school.

ANDREA   Hey, wait. Come on. It's Friday night. You gotta get out a little. Want me to come by and pick you up about seven? The game starts at seven-thirty. All the other kids are gonna be there.

GINA   Well, my dad's kinda funny. If I can come, I'll meet you there. Okay?

ANDREA   Okay, then. Bye. (*ANDREA walks on down the street. TONY and GINA approach their front door.*)

TONY   Why didn't you just tell her the truth? That dad's a mean drunk. Heck, we'll both be ninety before he lets us out of the house to be normal.

GINA   Shhh! He's sitting by the living room window. He'll hear you. Then we'll really catch it.

GINA, TONY, MOM, and DAD are seated around the dinner table. DAD has been drinking heavily. The nearly empty gin bottle sits in front of him.

DAD   How come you're all so quiet? A man who's worked hard all week likes to hear a little polite conversation. Know what I mean? Blasted spoiled kids anyway. You just sit there and slurp up the meal your mom has … Aw, heck, this was just a bunch of frozen stuff anyway, wasn't it?

GINA   Dad, Mom worked all week just like you did.

DAD   What? Are you talking back to me? You brat!

MOM   Honey, calm down.

DAD (*DAD slams his fist down on the table. His voice gets louder.*)   Don't tell me what to do! You know I can't stand people telling me what to do!

TONY   Dad, it's okay. We're not trying to tell you what to do.

MOM   Come on, you guys.

DAD   Come on nothing! These rotten kids make me sick! A man can't have peace in his own house. You brats clear this table right now and get to your rooms.

GINA   But Dad, I've gotta go down to the school tonight.

DAD (*He pours the rest of the gin into his glass and drinks it down while the others watch with expressionless faces. Finally, he leers around at them and speaks a bit slurred.*) Listen, young lady. You don't tell me what you're gonna do. I tell you. (*His voice raises.*) I tell you. You understand? (*He rises, knocking over the empty gin bottle. This makes him angrier.*) See what you made me do? Get to your rooms like I said!

TONY   That's not fair, Dad. We didn't do anything.

DAD   I'll decide what's fair around here. I'm still the man of this house.

GINA (*under her breath*)   A real man doesn't get drunk and yell at his family all the time.

MOM   Hush, Gina. You'll just make things worse. (*The two kids rise from the table and carry dishes to the sink.*)

DAD   What? What were you saying?

GINA   Nothing, Dad. We're going to our rooms now, like you said.

DAD   Good. It's about time. And I'll go watch the news and see what crap's going on in this sick world. What a life! (*He exits.*)

MOM   You guys finish cleaning up, will you? I've got a killer headache. (*She exits. They finish clearing the table. GINA runs the dishwater and begins washing the dishes. TONY dries them and puts them away.*)

TONY   Hey, we'll just wait till Dad falls asleep in front of the TV. Then we'll sneak on out of here out the back door. He'll never know we went to the game. Mom won't say anything.

GINA (*begins to cry softly*)   The whole thing just makes me sick. I'd have been out of here a long time ago if I weren't so worried about Mom.

TONY (*He puts his arm across her shoulder and gives her a gentle hug.*)   Hey, hey … come on. Freshen up and we'll get on down to the game. Maybe that someone who wants to meet you will be cool.

GINA (*She shakes her head.*)   I don't know how much longer I can stand this. Be quiet, or he'll hear us.

Discussion

1. What is the cause of the conflict in this family?
2. What agencies are in the school or community that could help with the problem?
3. What do you think keeps Mom, Gina, and Tony from leaving?
4. What has the mother done about the problem? What could she do?
5. What choices can Gina and Tony make that will help them deal with the problem most reasonably?
6. What would you do if you lived in that house?

Mom Didn't Mean to Hurt Me

CHARACTERS
CECELIA (age 11), BRAD (age 15), MOM, MR. MONTEZ, OFFICER JAMES

CECELIA and BRAD are sitting at the dinner table. MOM brings a platter of baked squash to the table and begins to place some on their plates.

BRAD   Mom, you know I don't like that stuff.

MOM (*Hesitates, stops and glares at him.*)   Listen, Brad, this isn't a restaurant. Besides, it's good for you. (*She sits down and picks up her fork.*)

CECELIA (*a snotty little sister*)   Yeah, Brad. I'd starve if I had to eat the dinner you *didn't* cook for us tonight.

BRAD (*He glares at her.*)   Shut up, you dork. Nobody asked for your opinion. (*under his breath*) What a boot licker!

CECELIA   Mom! Mom! Make him stop.

MOM (*Slams her fork down on the table.*)   Will you two both shut up? I'm so tired. Can't you just eat in peace, like a real family? (*They all eat quietly for a while.*)

BRAD (*He has pushed the squash to the side of the plate and eaten his ham slice and green beans.*)   Mom? Is there any more ham? I'm still hungry.

MOM (*getting angry*)   I gave you the biggest piece. And you haven't touched your squash. Eat your squash!

BRAD   Just forget it! (*He gets up from the table carrying his plate, stalks to the trash and dumps his squash, then slams his plate into the sink.*) I gotta finish my homework. (*He starts toward his room.*)

CECELIA (*trying to gain favor with her mother*)   Gee, Mom, I would have eaten his squash!

MOM (*really fed up now, yelling*)   Brad, get your butt back in here! (*She rises quickly from the table, tipping over her chair, louder.*) Brad, I said get your butt back here!

CECELIA (*becoming a little frightened*)   Uh-oh.

BRAD (*Appears in doorway to kitchen. His eyes are big and he's cowering.*)   I'm sorry, Mom. I'm sorry.

MOM (*yelling*)   Yes. You *are* sorry! (*She strides across the kitchen, grabs him by the hair, and yanks him across the room. He tries to grab her wrists, but she gets even angrier and completely loses control.*)

CECELIA   No, Mom! It's okay. He's sorry.

MOM   You stay out of this! (*With one hand still gripping BRAD's hair, she smacks him in the face hard with the other.*) How dare you talk to your mother like that! (*She smacks him again.*) You're just like your loser dad.

BRAD (*He crumples down to the floor with his arms covering his head.*)   I'm sorry, Mom. I'm sorry. (*He looks up at her.*) You didn't have to hit me.

MOM (*She stands up straight, stares down at him, then slowly turns away and slumps into her seat at the table.*)   Oh, God. What have I done?

CECELIA   It's okay, Mom. Here, I'll clear the table. (*She gets up and begins to carry dishes to the sink.*)

MOM (*Turning to look at BRAD who has gotten up, is standing, and touching a quickly swelling eye.*)   Oh, my God. I'm so sorry, Son. (*She rises.*) Here, let me get some ice to put on that.

BRAD   No. I'll get it. (*She freezes and watches him helplessly. He grabs a plastic bag out of a drawer, goes to the refrigerator, gets ice, and gingerly places the bag on his eye.*) I better go finish my homework. (*He exits.*)

CECELIA   Are you going to let him go to school tomorrow if he has another black eye?

Two days later, BRAD is sitting in math class. His eye has turned an ugly purple. MR. MONTEZ notices.

MR. MONTEZ   Brad? Is that a black eye? Look at me, Son.

BRAD (*grins, trying to downplay the situation*)   It's nothing, Mr. Montez.

MR. MONTEZ   That's the third one you've had. You do know, don't you, that repeated blows to the head can cause permanent brain damage?

BRAD   Yeah, I've heard that.

MR. MONTEZ   Do you want to tell me what happened?

BRAD (*knowing that MR. MONTEZ won't let it rest*)   Oh, I just got to fooling around … and I crashed my bike. (*pause*) Clumsy, huh? It runs in the family.

MR. MONTEZ (*frowning*)   You have a lot of accidents, Brad. (*pause*) We've got to get the lesson started now, but I'll talk to you more about this later.

MR. MONTEZ, OFFICER JAMES, and BRAD are seated in an office at school. MR. MONTEZ has paperwork in front of him.

BRAD (*nervously, to MR. MONTEZ*)   You didn't need to call him in, Mr. Montez. I told you it was nothing.

MR. MONTEZ   I'm worried about you, Brad. You've had too many black eyes, and I've noticed bruises on your wrists and arms, like someone was yanking you around. By law, I've got to report anything that makes me think you might be being hurt at home.

BRAD (*looking down and fiddling with his fingers*)   Oh, God.

OFFICER JAMES   So that's why your teacher called me in here today. We want to do the right thing. Let me look at your eye. (*He peers at BRAD'S eye a minute.*) So you say you crashed on your bike? That doesn't look right. That looks like someone hit you real hard across the face.

MR. MONTEZ   The first time, I figured boys will be boys, but the second time, I began to be suspicious that a pattern was forming. This third time, I couldn't let it slide. I am going to have to fill out a report of possible child abuse.

BRAD (*Looks back and forth between them, pleading.*)   I don't want my mom getting in trouble. She just loses it sometimes. I get on her nerves, you know. (*MR. MONTEZ and OFFICER JAMES just look at him knowingly.*)

OFFICER JAMES   The law is in place to protect kids. If your mom is stressed out, then she needs help. I'm going to have to pass this on to Child Protective Services. They'll be checking into your situation.

BRAD   You don't have to do that. I promise, I won't get on her nerves anymore.

OFFICER JAMES   Sorry, Brad.

Discussion

1. Do you think Brad's mom loves him? Do you think Brad loves his mom?
2. Why do you think Brad's mom loses control of her temper? Give all the reasons you can think of.
3. Why do you think Brad was disrespectful to his mom? What would you have done?
4. Should Mr. Montez have gotten involved? What would you have done?
5. What would be the best outcome for this situation?

I Can't Live in This House

CHARACTERS
  VANESSA, CARLTON and CAMILLA (boyfriend and girlfriend), MOM, DAD,
  MRS. GIBSON (teacher), MRS. RUDOLPH (sexual assault speaker)

CARLTON and CAMILLA are driving VANESSA home after school.

CARLTON Vanessa, your house is up around this corner coming up, right?

VANESSA (*rather subdued*) Uh, yeah, take a left at the stop sign.

CAMILLA You sound kinda down. Is something the matter?

VANESSA No, not really. I just get tired of my mom working four to midnight. I have to get dinner and clean up by myself.

CAMILLA Really? Doesn't your dad help you?

VANESSA No. (*She doesn't want to talk to them about her family.*)

They pull up in front of Vanessa's house. She hesitates getting out of the car. Finally, she shoves the door open, steps out, turns and pushes the door shut.

CARLTON Well, you're home safe, at least. Take care now. (*He and CAMILLA drive off. VANESSA waves as she watches them round the corner.*)

VANESSA (*to herself*) Yeah, sure. Safe. Right! I hope he's not home. (*She turns and approaches the front door, then pauses as she sees DAD standing in the kitchen watching her out the window.*) Oh no. (*VANESSA opens the door and enters the hallway. DAD approaches her and tries to give her a hug.*)

DAD There's my baby. (*She squirms away from him.*) Hey, don't be like that. What're you so up tight for? Come on, give your daddy a kiss.

VANESSA Dad, please? Please? I don't like it when you grab on me like that.

DAD (*He's becoming angry.*) So! Getting all uppity, are you? Is that what they're teaching you at that high school? How to disrespect your own father?

VANESSA No, Dad. (*He grabs her and pulls her to him.*) Please don't, Dad. Please?

DAD After all the things I've bought for you? You owe me a little affection, Baby.

VANESSA Dad, please don't call me Baby. I'm too old for that. (*under her breath*) Why don't you talk to Mom about your need for affection, you pig!

DAD What did you say? (*He shoves her away.*) You better keep your mouth shut to your mom, you understand! You are just as guilty as I am. You know you liked it. (*He softens and tries to pull her back up against him.*) You know how much I love you, Baby.

VANESSA (*Pushing away again and trying to change the subject.*) Dad, I thought you worked late tonight.

DAD (*ignoring her effort*) Yeah. I guess you are getting too old and sophisticated for your poor old dad. How about just once more, for old time's sake, and then I won't ask you anymore?

VANESSA Dad, how come you're not still at work? Please, no more, Dad. No. It's not right. I don't like this.

At school the next day, VANESSA comes in looking very dejected. She smiles out of habit at MRS. GIBSON, her health teacher. CARLTON and CAMILLA also share health class.

MRS. GIBSON Hey, Vanessa. How're you doing today? Are you okay? You look a little tired.

VANESSA   Yeah, I'm really tired. I didn't sleep well last night.

MRS. GIBSON   Oh, too much TV, huh? (*She laughs, trying to cheer VANESSA up.*)

VANESSA   Yeah, sure. (*trying to change the subject*) Are we having a guest speaker today? You said yesterday that unless there was an emergency, that someone was coming in to talk to us about … sex.

CARLTON   Hey, that sounds good. (*A few students laugh.*)

CAMILLA (*to CARLTON*)   You just had to say that, didn't you? (*She rolls her eyes and smiles.*)

MRS. GIBSON   Yes, I did say we were going to have a guest speaker. But it's not going to be funny. It's about sexual assault. Mrs. Rudolph is from Sexual Assault Services. She'll be talking about sex crimes, rape, incest, and so forth. I don't think you'll be bored. (*Pause; the classroom door opens and in steps Mrs. Rudolph.*) Oh, here she is now. Come on in. Let me introduce you to health class.

MRS. RUDOLPH   Well, hi, students. It's a pleasure to be here. If my beeper goes off, I may have to stop and make a call. You see, I'm on duty right now to help people who've been victims of a sex crime. So, I'll get right into the subject.

CARLTON   With all due respect, Ma'am, how can sex be a crime? I mean, I know about the rapists who snatch girls off the street, but that's different.

MRS. RUDOLPH   Good question, young man. A sex crime happens anytime someone uses power to force sexual contact with someone else who doesn't want it. It can be a boyfriend forcing his girlfriend into sex even though she doesn't want to go all the way, or it can be just guys or girls grabbing on each other's private parts any time and any place when that grabbing isn't wanted. And it can even happen in families when older members look for sexual fulfillment with younger members, like with older brothers fooling around with their sisters, or when fathers or even mothers, use their own children for sexual pleasure.

CAMILLA Oh, gosh. That makes me sick. People don't talk about it much. I know it happens. But what can anyone do about it? (*VANESSA puts her head down on the desk and closes her eyes.*)

MRS. RUDOLPH   Well, it is a serious crime. When it's reported, if it goes to court, it can break up a home. And a lot of time, if adults are preying on children, they threaten them that if they tell, they'll go to hell, or be killed, or their other family members will be killed. It puts a terrible burden on children. They think it's their fault. (*She looks around the room and sees a lot of serious faces.*) I just want to say this to all of you here today. It is *never* the victim's fault. Especially a child's.

VANESSA   That makes me sick. I think punks that do that to children should be killed! (*The class laughs nervously.*)

MRS. GIBSON   Yes, we can understand your feelings. And killings have happened over this crime. But it's very hard for a victim of incest. In case some of you might not know, incest is sex by another family member. It's hard for them to come forward, isn't it, Mrs. Rudolph?

MRS. RUDOLPH   Yes, it is. And that's why it's so important for me to talk to you today about this. Children need love from their parents. And they're dependent for food and shelter. When a child is sexually used by a parent, that child feels terrible conflict. They love their parent, but in their guts, they know that what is going on is wrong. Often, they blame themselves. (*pause*) Our agency, Sexual Assault Services, is here to help you. We are available 24 hours a day to talk to you. We keep what you say confidential. We know the law and will help someone press charges, if they wish. We go to court with the victims, and we offer individual and group counseling free. Young lady (*She points to VANESSA.*), would you be willing to hand this flyer out to everyone in the class for me? (*VANESSA gets up and begins to pass the flyers out.*) Even if someone doesn't want to press charges, talking often helps a lot. We're here to help.

CARLTON   You act like some of us might really need this. Do you know something we don't know? (*He laughs.*)

MRS. RUDOLPH   Relax. I don't know any of your personal business, but I do know that more than half of all young women have had unwanted sexual contact. And boys are not exempt. The figures suggest that four out of ten boys have also been victims. Remember, any type of forced sexual touch is sexual assault. (*Her beeper goes off.*) Uh-oh. I'm sorry. I was afraid of that. I'll have to go now, but I invite you to call that number on the flyer. And tell all your friends, too. (*exits*)

Saturday morning in living room of VANESSA'S house. She and MOM are watching TV.

MOM   Vanessa, give me the remote. I can't stand watching these brainless cartoons. I can't vacuum until your dad wakes up.

VANESSA (*handing MOM the remote*)   Uh, Mom? Can I talk to you a minute?

MOM (*MOM mutes the TV and turns toward VANESSA.*)   What is it, honey?

VANESSA   Uh, Mom, I've gotta talk to you about Dad. (*pause*) I don't want to be alone with him in the evenings any more. Can you please just work days instead?

MOM   Whatever for, Vanessa? You know I get time and a half for working evenings. We need the money. (*pause*) What is it, honey? Has your dad been mean to you?

VANESSA   Mom, it's more than that. I hate to mention this, but … oh, never mind.

MOM   No, honey. What is it? (*She is becoming concerned.*) What is it?

VANESSA   It's so ugly. I'm ashamed to even mention it.

MOM   What, honey? Just come out with it.

VANESSA   Mom, he's been messing with me when you're not home.

MOM   Messing with you! Vanessa, what are you saying? Are you saying he's been touching you wrong? You know, your private places?

VANESSA (*softly, but relieved that her mother knows*)   Yes. Even more than just touching. Everything. It's been going on since I was nine. He threatened to leave you if I said anything. He said he'd take me away and I'd never see you again. He said it was because he loved me so much.

MOM   Oh, no. Oh, no. How much did he hurt you? My baby!

VANESSA   Mom, don't call me your baby. That's what he calls me. I can't stand it any more. It was all I could do to come home last night. I can't live here with him in the house anymore. (*She begins to cry.*)

Discussion

1. What is Mom's conflict? What choices does she have now? What should she do?
2. Should Vanessa have told her mother? What choices does she have if her mother won't help her?
3. Why do you think the father would want to have sex with his own daughter?
4. What should happen to the father? Name all the possibilities.
5. What are the best ways to help all three members of this family?

You Gotta Learn to Live With People Like That!

CHARACTERS
BRIAN, MARTIN, DAVID, COACH CHENEY (gym teacher), MOM, DAD

In the locker area in gym class, DAVID and MARTIN approach BRIAN to bully him.

MARTIN   Hey, punk! (*giving BRIAN a shove*) We told you to get out of here.

DAVID   Yeah, what're you doing, spying on us?

BRIAN   What are you talking about?

MARTIN (*giving BRIAN another shove*)   Hey, we ask the questions here. (*DAVID slams BRIAN's locker shut.*)

DAVID   Now get out, or do you want us to put you out?

BRIAN (*realizing it's two against one*)   Okay, okay. I'm going. (*He hurries out.*)

Out on the athletic field, COACH CHENEY is taking roll.

COACH CHENEY   Martin Locksley? (*no answer*) Martin? Anybody seen him? I thought I saw him here today.

BRIAN   Yeah, I saw him. He was still in the locker room.

COACH CHENEY (*looking up and studying BRIAN's face*)   You saw him in there? Okay, thanks.

COACH CHENEY continues with roll call, then tells his assistant to get the students started on the volleyball courts. He goes back into the locker room and catches MARTIN and DAVID rifling through someone else's locker. He calls for school security, and soon the two boys are in the office being suspended. Later that night, the phone at BRIAN's house rings. DAD picks it up.

DAD   Hello? Yes, Brian Jenkins lives here. (*pause*) You want to talk to him? (*pause*) May I tell him who's calling? (*pause*) Okay, just a minute. (*He sets the phone down.*) Hey, Brian, some guy's on the phone for you. Says he has a class with you.

BRIAN   Okay. Thanks, Dad. (*He picks up the phone.*) Hello? (*pause*) Hello? (*He jerks the phone away from his ear.*) Gosh, that's weird. (*He hangs up the phone.*)

MOM (*has been watching from the couch*)   What's weird, honey?

BRIAN   It's nothing, Mom. Just some crazy creep on the line playing a joke.

MOM   Well, what did they say?

BRIAN   They didn't really say anything. But there were some really loud bangs into the receiver.

MOM   Bangs? Like what? Not gunshots, I hope.

BRIAN   It was a joke, Mom. Just forget it.

In gym locker room several days later after MARTIN and DAVID have been allowed back in school.

MARTIN   Hey, David, here he is!

DAVID   Who? That punk? Is this a good time to get him?

MARTIN (*looking around*)   Yeah. Most everyone's already out.

BRIAN (*Already heading for the door, he sees them coming toward him.*)   Uh-oh. What do you guys want now? I'm on my way out.

MARTIN   You punk! You squealed on us. We got suspended.

DAVID (*grabbing BRIAN'S t-shirt and shoving him backward*)   Yeah. Didn't you get our phone message?

BRIAN (*struggling to get away*)   Yeah, I got it. What're you after me for? I didn't do anything.

MARTIN   You told the teacher we were still in the locker room. We got suspended because of you. Now you're gonna pay! (*He socks BRIAN'S jaw hard.*)

BRIAN   Hey, man, lay off! (*DAVID punches him in the stomach. BRIAN sags down, his back against the wall, with the wind knocked out of him. A voice yells, "Here comes the coach!"*)

DAVID (*to MARTIN*)   Outta here, man. This way. (*They head for the emergency exit.*)

MARTIN (*yelling back at BRIAN*)   Keep your mouth shut this time, punk.

COACH CHENEY (*entering locker room*)   Hey, hold it! What's going on in here? (*noticing BRIAN crumpled against the wall*) Oh, no! What's this? Brian! What happened?

BRIAN (*Looking up, then reaching up to touch his bruised and swelling cheek. He struggles to get up. COACH CHENEY pulls him up by the arm.*)   Uh, I'm okay, I think.

COACH CHENEY   Well, let's get you to the office. We've got to get some ice on your face right away. (*They begin to head out of the locker room toward the office.*) Who did this to you anyway?

BRIAN   I don't know. It happened so fast, I didn't recognize them.

COACH CHENEY   Don't want to tell me, huh?

BRIAN's DAD was called to the school to pick him up. They are in the car on the way home. His dad is angry.

DAD   I hope I never have to do this again! It's downright embarrassing to have to pick your kid up from school because he couldn't stand up to some bullies! What'sa matter with you anyway? My own son's a pansy.

BRIAN   Dad, it wasn't like that. They ganged up on me.

DAD   Yeah, sure. You knew something was up and you just let it happen. Your mom told me about the gunshot noises on the phone.

BRIAN   Dad, all I did was tell Coach that Martin was still in the locker room. What's so wrong about that? I haven't done anything wrong.

DAD   So, you "told" Coach on them? No wonder they're mad. You gotta learn to mind your own business. And if you have to, you make *them* afraid of you. I can't believe you were such a pansy. Good thing your grandpa's not still alive to see me dragging my little boy home from school because some punk punched him and he didn't even fight back. Just shut up, will you?

BRIAN   Dad, that's not fair. I don't think it's cool to be a fighter. I don't want to get kicked out. I want to graduate.

DAD   Hey, first things first. You gotta learn to be a man first.

Discussion

1. Name all the ways you can think of that Brian could deal with Martin and David.
2. Should he file a complaint against them for assault? Why or why not?
3. What can he do about his dad? Why do you think his dad doesn't worry more about Brian's safety?
4. How should Brian best handle this situation? How can school authorities help him?
5. What would you do to help Brian if you were the school counselor?

Dad Says to Win Any Way You Can

CHARACTERS

   LENNY, DAD, BEATRICE, MR. BRAME (history teacher), MRS. HOWELL (principal)

LENNY and BEATRICE are studying in the public library.

LENNY   Hey, Beatrice, do you have your report ready for Mr. Brame on Friday?

BEATRICE   Oh, man, that's what I've been working on. I picked the Civil Rights Act. I got some stuff off the internet, but I'm not quite done yet. I think I'll be done on time. What about you?

LENNY   Wow. Well, I'm not in such good shape. In fact, I haven't even started. I don't know what I'm going to do. I gotta do this to keep a C average so I can stay on the team. You got any good ideas?

BEATRICE   Like what? You either work your hind end off and do the work or you don't. What's your subject?

LENNY   Well, I don't even have any ideas. You got any suggestions?

BEATRICE   Hmmm. It has to be about our civil rights. How about one of the Bill of Rights? Like maybe the fourth. You know, the one about unreasonable searches. You oughta care about that. Like if a cop pulls you over, when can they search your car? Or searches in schools? You could find out how the courts have determined these should be. (*pause*) Uh-oh. I see your eyes are glazing over.

LENNY   This sounds like work. I think I'd rather go mow the lawn.

BEATRICE   Oh, please! Hey, being a high school graduate should mean you know something about our country.

LENNY   Now you really sound like Mr. Brame. (*pause*) Hey, I gotta go. (*He rises to leave.*) I'll ask my dad to help get me out of this mess.

BEATRICE (*frowning*)   Not going to do the sweat, huh? (*She turns back to her report.*)

Later, in the garage, LENNY approaches his DAD, who is changing the spark plugs on the pickup.

LENNY   Whatcha doing, Dad?

DAD (*looking up and wiping his handkerchief across his eyes*)   Oh, there you are. I was going to ask you to finish this for me. Where you been?

LENNY   I been at practice and the library, Dad. But one problem.

DAD   What's that? Is your ankle okay? I thought that was all healed up.

LENNY   No, it's not that, Dad. It's my U.S. History class. I'm gonna get a D unless I get a big old report done for Friday. Mr. Brame will see I'm disqualified from playing Friday night. I gotta get the thing done, but it's so boring.

DAD   So when did you know about this report?

LENNY   Uh, he told us about it the first week of the class. I've just been busy.

DAD   That figures. So what's today? (*He looks at his calendar watch.*) Wednesday. Hmmm. How much do you have done?

LENNY   Well, I picked the subject.

DAD   Hey, that's good. (*He pauses and scratches his head.*) What is it?

LENNY   Uh, this girl, you know, a brainy type, well she said maybe I could do it on the fourth one of the Bill of Rights. I think she said it was about searches. I do know the report has to be about our rights.

DAD   Well, there's a way out. I'll tell you what I think we can do. You gotta stay on the team. I got a tip that a scout from state college was going to be there. You gotta look good.

LENNY   So what's your idea, Dad?

DAD   Well, Bob down at work, says on the internet, you can get whole papers. You know, just copy them off and hand them in. Your teacher won't be able to trace it. You'll be home free. I'll give him a call right now if you'll finish those spark plugs for me. Okay?

LENNY   Hey, cool, Dad. Hand me that wrench, will you? (*He grabs the wrench and bends over the engine.*)

DAD   I'll be back in a few. (*exits*)

LENNY works on the spark plugs. DAD comes back into the garage in a few minutes.

LENNY   So, what did he say?

DAD   You're home free, Son. He'll bring it to work tomorrow. You can have it ready to turn in Friday. I told him I'd buy him all the hot dogs he could eat at the game. He wants to see you play, too.

In class, Friday morning, LENNY hands the report to MR. BRAME.

MR. BRAME   Thank you very much, Lenny. I was hoping I wouldn't have to disqualify you for tonight's game. I know it means a lot to you.

LENNY (*grinning sheepishly*)   A man's gotta do what a man's gotta do, Mr. Brame.

MR. BRAME (*looking intently into LENNY'S face*)   Yes. That's right. I'm looking forward to reading your opinions. (*He glances at the title, then frowns slightly.*) Hmmm. I see your report is on the Fourth Amendment. Yes, I suppose teens would be very interested in that. Especially concerning school authorities' rights to search students. You did mention that in here, I hope.

LENNY (*looking around nervously*)   Uh, sure. That's an important issue. (*The bell rings to sit down.*) Uh-oh. I better sit down. Uh, there's no hurry for you to read that, Mr. Brame.

Later that day, Lenny sits in the principal's office facing MR. BRAME and MRS. HOWELL.

MRS. HOWELL   Well, Lenny. I'm really disappointed in you. Can you guess why?

LENNY (*looking at the floor, then resigning himself*)   What seems to be the matter?

MRS. HOWELL   Lenny, personal honesty seems to be at stake here. I'd like you to come clean with us.

LENNY   About what?

MR. BRAME   I think you know, Lenny. Please respect us enough to tell us the truth.

LENNY   About what? What are you talking about? (*MRS. HOWELL holds up his report. Across the top is written "Plagiarized—F." LENNY looks at it, turns red, then throws up his hands.*) You don't want me to play tonight, do you? What do you have against me anyway? My dad is right. This school is a bunch of uppity geeks. Man, I just want to play ball. I don't need all this school stuff. I don't see how it's going to help me as an athlete. (*He shakes his head.*) This sucks.

MRS. HOWELL   Lenny, we have no choice. You're off the team. For how long depends on you. Believe me, we're just as disappointed as you are that you can't play tonight because the team needs you. But even worse, we're disappointed that you cheated.

Discussion

1. What are Lenny's conflicts in this story? Do you think he realized that plagiarism is cheating?
2. What is the best way the dad could have helped his son?
3. What is wrong with plagiarism or other cheating?
4. Did Mr. Brame do the right thing by turning Lenny in when he realized that Lenny had cheated? Explain.
5. Should the school allow Lenny to make up for his cheating so that he can earn his way back on the team?
6. If you were the principal, what would you do?

You Can Let Me Off on This Corner

CHARACTERS

TERRI, SAMANTHA, WALTER, MRS. JEFFERSON (teacher)

TERRI and her mother live in a run-down apartment complex. Trash litters the grounds. Inside their apartment, they sleep on mattresses on the floor without sheets and pillows. TERRI's mom works part-time as a stocker in a grocery warehouse, so to help feed them, she brings home food that is supposed to go in the dumpster. TERRI struggles to find suitable clothes to wear to school. TERRI sits on her mattress with her back against the wall. She is writing in a journal.

TERRI (*TERRI's voice speaks what is written in her journal.*)   "I feel very sad today. Mom didn't get the check from Dad again this month, so we'll be lucky to get the rent money. I don't dare ask her if I can get something to wear on the field trip. Mrs. Jefferson said to try to dress up because we'll be visiting businesses and we should look good to represent the school. I better not even tell Mom that I'm worried about it, because she'll start crying again. I gave her the fifteen dollars I earned baby-sitting, but that had to go on the gas bill, she said. So maybe I better not go." (*TERRI closes the journal and stares straight ahead.*)

The next day in class, MRS. JEFFERSON is reminding students to bring her their permission slips for the trip.

MRS. JEFFERSON   So did anyone else remember their permission slip? The trip is this Friday. Let's see here. (*She checks her list.*) Terri? Where's yours? You are going with us, aren't you?

TERRI   Uh, no, I can't go, Mrs. Jefferson. Sorry.

MRS. JEFFERSON   That doesn't seem right. Would you stay a moment after class? I'd like to try to work something out so you can go. The business department's been planning this trip for a long time.

The bell for class dismissal rings.

SAMANTHA (*to the girl sitting next to her but loud enough for TERRI and MRS. JEFFERSON to hear*)   That girl doesn't have anything to wear, I bet.

MRS. JEFFERSON (*realizing that this may be TERRI's real reason for not wanting to go on the trip*)   Terri?

TERRI (*approaches MRS. JEFFERSON's desk*)   You wanted to speak to me?

MRS. JEFFERSON   Terri, I really want you to be able to go with us on the trip. (*She looks around to make sure the other students have all gone.*) Listen, I notice you wear the same things to school a lot. Now don't be embarrassed.

TERRI   Yeah, I was hoping nobody'd notice. It's true. I don't have anything to wear. I can't ask my mom to get me anything right now. Thanks anyway. Maybe next time. (*She heads for the door.*)

MRS. JEFFERSON   Wait, Terri. Listen, my daughter's about your size. She's got a couple of outfits she doesn't wear anymore. Let me bring them for you tomorrow. Nobody else will ever know. Please let me do this for you. You need to go on this trip.

TERRI (*realizing she will hurt the teacher's feelings if she doesn't accept and really wanting the clothes*)   Well, okay. That's really nice of you. Gosh, I don't know what to say.

Terri and the others are on the bus on their way to the business they will visit as a part of the field trip. Terri is dressed in a sharp outfit.

WALTER (*seated behind TERRI*)   So what's up, Terri? I've never seen you dressed up before. You look all business-like. And if you don't mind my saying it, really nice.

TERRI (*Turns around and sees him smiling at her. She blushes.*)   Well, thanks. I don't want to disgrace our beloved school.

WALTER   Hey, I see you walking home from school everyday. Maybe I could give you a ride home today. It wouldn't be cool to get all sweaty in that outfit.

TERRI (*pleased at the attention but a little embarrassed*)   Oh, you don't need to do that. I just tell my feet where to go and then just sit back and enjoy the trip.

WALTER (*He smiles at her evasiveness.*)   Well, think about it. I'll check with you when we get back.

After the trip, the students are getting off the bus. SAMANTHA approaches WALTER.

SAMANTHA   Hey, wait up, Walter. Can you give me a lift home? My mom's still at work.

WALTER   Sure, I guess so. Just a minute. (*calling after TERRI who is starting down the street*) Hey, Terri? Hold up. (*He catches up to her.*) Hey, come on. Let me give you a ride home. It's still too hot for you to walk.

TERRI   Oh, hi. I thought you were with Samantha. It's okay. I walk home everyday.

WALTER   No, Terri, come on. We're all just friends. Let me give you a lift. Come on. I even just washed my car.

In the car, Terri sits in the passenger seat.

WALTER   So where's your house, Terri? I know it's in this direction.

TERRI (*not wanting the kids to know where she lives*)   Oh, keep going. I'll let you know when to let me out. I can walk the rest of the way.

WALTER   Hey, no. I'll take you all the way home. I've got lots of gas. Let's just say I want to do a good deed today.

TERRI (*trying to act casual*)   What're you saying? You're a Boy Scout and I'm a little old lady you've got to help across the street? (*They all laugh.*)

SAMANTHA   Oh, Terri. It's okay. He likes to be seen with a car full of girls.

TERRI (*Desperate that they won't see where she really lives, she asks WALTER to drive up the wrong street with nice apartments.*)   All right. Turn at left at the next corner and up two blocks. It's in the Broadway Village complex.

WALTER   Okay, here we are. (*WALTER lets her out in front of the classy entrance to the complex.*) See you Monday.

SAMANTHA (*calling out the car window*)   Hey, nice place. Bye. See you.

TERRI waves at them as they turn the corner and leave the area. Then she turns and walks an extra six blocks home.

Discussion

1. Why did Terry lie to the kids about where she lived?
2. Do you think Walter and Samantha would have thought less of Terri if they had seen where she really lived?
3. Name all the ways, both bad and good, that Terri could deal with her problems.
4. Who would be helped or hurt by these choices?
5. What do you think is the best way for Terri to deal with her problems?
6. If you were in a similar situation, what would you do?

PART II: FRIENDS AND ACQUAINTANCES

What's a real friend do?

Skit 13

She's Been Acting Really Weird

CHARACTERS
MARLA, CAROLE, ESTHER, DEVIN, MR. BAILEY

MARLA is home alone. She has been drinking and writing in her journal.

MARLA (*She reads aloud from the journal.*) "This whole life sucks. Mom won't let me see Devin any more because she thinks he slinks around. She doesn't know that he actually listens to me when I talk and cares what I think. She thinks because he's older, he just wants me as a little plaything. It's none of her business who I go out with." (*The phone rings.*) Hello? Devin! Oh, my God, it's so good to hear your voice.

DEVIN (*voice on phone*) Hey, princess. Is your mom home?

MARLA Not right now. She went to a class at the college. She'll be home around ten.

DEVIN So we can talk a while then?

MARLA Oh, yes. I was just writing in my diary how depressed I am about how things are. I won't be eighteen for two more years, so I have to do what she says unless I run away.

DEVIN No, girl, you don't want to do that. The streets are rough, believe me.

MARLA Maybe we could go somewhere, you know, like Romeo and Juliet.

DEVIN That wouldn't be so good with you being only sixteen. They'd claim I kidnapped a minor. But if your mom won't be back for a while, I could sneak in your window for a while. You sound a little funny. You been drinking?

MARLA Well, without you, I've been spending a little time with Jack Daniels. But it hasn't helped much. Just makes me more depressed. As for you sneaking over, it's already nine. It's too much of a risk for tonight. Besides, last time, you didn't bring a condom. And you promised me.

DEVIN Hey, when a guy loves a girl so much, he wants everything to be natural, you know?

MARLA I love to hear you say that.

DEVIN What? The natural part?

MARLA No, the "guy loves a girl so much" part. (*The front door opens and closes.*) Uh-oh. Someone's here. I think my mom came home early. I've gotta go. Stop by the school and we can talk a little while in your car, okay?

The next day MARLA is sitting in math class beside her friend CAROLE. CAROLE whispers to her.

CAROLE You look kinda strung out today. Are you okay?

MARLA Barely. Jack Daniels got me through the night. You know my mom won't let me see Devin. She checks up on me all the time. But he might stop by outside the school today.

CAROLE That's what I wanted to talk to you about.

MR. BAILEY Ladies, please. Could you pay attention? I'm almost done explaining these problems. And Marla, you need all the help you can get.

The girls are silent while MR. BAILEY finishes his teaching. MARLA's face turns red because the teacher identified her in front of the whole class as needing lots of help. When he finishes, CAROLE goes to his desk.

CAROLE   Uh, Mr. Bailey, could Marla and I go outside and talk privately a few minutes? She's kinda upset about something.

MR. BAILEY   If you must. But don't be long. (*CAROLE beckons MARLA to accompany her out the door; to MARLA.*) Don't be long now. You flunked that last test. Even community college won't want you with the GPA you're earning.

MARLA   I know, Mr. Bailey. You don't need to broadcast it to the whole class.

MR. BAILEY   And you don't need to be snippy about it!

Outside the room, they wait till nobody is near.

MARLA   So, what's so important? You're making me nervous.

CAROLE   I hate to tell you this because I know you're feeling really down, but you shouldn't trust Devin too much.

MARLA   What are you talking about? Gosh, nobody wants me to be happy.

CAROLE   No, Marla. Listen. It's better you know. Several of us have seen him hanging around that girl Esther. You know, that real pretty girl who works at K-Mart.

MARLA   So? Maybe she's his sister.

CAROLE   Well, if she is, he made her pregnant. My mom works there too, and she told her that Devin was so proud she was going to have his son. They're looking for a place to move in together.

MARLA   You're lying. (*She begins to cry.*) No, I *wish* you were lying. Oh, God, now what will I do?

CAROLE   Just forget about his scuzzy butt. He's not worth one tear of yours.

MARLA   But he took something very precious of mine.

CAROLE   Oh, no, girl. You don't mean …

MARLA   Yes, I do. Now I'm not worth anything to anybody.

CAROLE   Don't talk that way. This isn't some old-time culture where women are just property.

MARLA   That's not what my mom thinks. (*CAROLE gives her a hug.*)

MR. BAILEY (*stepping out the door to check on them*)   What's going on out here? It's time to get back in and do your work. I bet you're crying over some boy. Snap out of it. You can do that on your own time. (*They all go back in the room, but MARLA spends the rest of the period scribbling doodles in her notebook.*)

MARLA avoids DEVIN after school that day by sneaking out the back of the campus and walking home along different streets.

MARLA (*sitting on her bed reading aloud from her journal*)   "So I'm flunking math. Devin has another girl pregnant, and I feel like such a jerk. In two weeks, I'll be seventeen, and I bet my dad won't even remember my birthday. I hate to admit it, but Mom was right about Devin being a slink. And I fell for it. I wish Mom wasn't so busy with her job and going to school. Carole's all right to talk to, but she doesn't want to hear my troubles all the time. But anyway, I've got Jack." (*She pours a small glass full from the bottle on her nightstand and drinks it down.*) "I wonder if I drank enough and passed out, I'd see that white light that people talk about where you get swallowed up in it and feels so good and peaceful and full of love." (*She drinks another glass full.*)

A few days later after school, MARLA goes into the K-Mart where ESTHER works. ESTHER is in the linen section stocking towels.

MARLA   You like working here?

ESTHER   It's okay, but I'm going to quit soon. You can see I'm going to have a baby. I'm so happy.

MARLA   Really? That's good, I guess, if the baby's father is happy too.

ESTHER   Oh, he is. He loves me very much. And we're moving in together. We're going to get married after my son is born.

MARLA   You must love him very much. The father, I mean.

ESTHER   Oh, yes. He's the best thing that's ever happened to me.

MARLA   (*turning away*)   Good for you. Some guys are such skunks.

After school the next day, MARLA has gotten her math test back with an F. CAROLE invites her to go for a soda. They are facing each other across the table.

CAROLE   So, it looks like you've gotten over that scuzzy guy Devin. I told you he was a loser.

MARLA   Yeah, well I guess losers attract losers. I got the F in math. My dad can't make it for my birthday, and my mom is really busy with her job and school. I guess this is what life is all about. No wonder people get a smile on their faces when they see the white light.

CAROLE   What are you talking about?

MARLA   You know, when they are dying, a white light appears and they go into it, and all they feel is love. That sounds so good. I'm so tired of struggling. In fact, I brought with me my lucky Teddy bear my dad gave me when I was three. I used to sleep with it every night. (*She gets it out of her backpack and hands it to CAROLE.*) Here, I want you to have it. You're my best friend, and I know you'll take good care of it.

CAROLE   No, girl. (*Hands the bear back.*) What are you talking about? We had a speaker in health class the other day that talked about when people are thinking of ending it all. Marla, are you thinking about that?

MARLA   Hey, why not? It would be better for everybody. I'm such a burden to my mom.

CAROLE   Hey, now don't talk that way. But tell me how you feel. Do you have a plan, a way to do it?

MARLA   Well, I could sneak some of my mom's sleeping pills and then have a long talk with Jack Daniels. I heard some famous old movie star did it that way once.

CAROLE   Oh, God. Marla, you're scaring me. Don't you realize that suicide is a permanent end to a temporary problem? That's what the speaker said. You're only sixteen. You can't do this. Don't you know people care about you?

MARLA   You say that, but how come I don't feel it? I just can't face another day of being such a wreck.

Discussion

1. Should Carole have told Marla that Devin was cheating on her? Why or why not?
2. How is Marla using liquor to handle her problems?
3. Should Marla be expected to know how to handle her problems? Why or why not?
4. Do other kids have problems as bad or even worse? Explain.
5. Without abusing substances or hurting herself, what could she do to overcome her depression?
6. According to the warning signs of suicide, how serious is Marla? What signs has she given that she is really thinking about it?
7. What should Carole do next to help her friend? Should she try to handle it all by herself?
8. What agencies in the school or community could help Marla?
9. If Marla were to commit suicide, who would be hurt? Who would be to blame?
10. If Marla were your friend, what would you do next?

She's Just Not Feeling Well

CHARACTERS

SHARI, AUDRA, KARLTON, PAUL, MR. RICH

Students are gathered in a recreation area during a ten-minute break between classes.

PAUL (*sipping from a soft drink bottle*) Man, this stuff'll give you a buzz. (*to SHARI*) Want a sip? It tastes pretty good.

SHARI What's in it? (*She takes the bottle and sniffs it.*) It just smells like orange soda. Are you sure it's okay? I don't want to get silly.

PAUL No, you don't want to make anyone suspicious. A few kids could get in serious trouble. Hey, it's safe. I'm okay. Try it. Just a little taste won't kill you.

SHARI Yeah, I guess so. (*She takes two swallows.*) Hmmm. Not bad. Care if I have one more sip?

PAUL Go for it, girl. Someone else gave it to me.

AUDRA (*approaching SHARI*) Hey, girl, what are you doing?

SHARI (*giggling*) Oh, hi, Audra. (*points to PAUL*) This guy gave me something to quench my thirst, you know what I mean. (*holds up the bottle*) See, it's orange soda.

AUDRA Yeah, okay. But it's almost time for English class. We better get going. We get to watch the end of that film, you know, *Lord of the Flies.*

SHARI Oh, that's right. (*turning to PAUL*) Hey, I gotta go. (*hands him the bottle*) Thanks. (*Both girls exit.*)

PAUL Okay. I guess I'll just have to have my own private little party by myself. (*spots KARLTON and approaches him*) Hey, man, want a sip of this? It's good stuff, if you know what I mean. It'll help get you through the afternoon.

KARLTON (*knowingly*) Just orange soda, huh?

PAUL Yeah, sure it is. But it's better than plain. Here. Drink up. (*extends bottle toward KARLTON*)

KARLTON No, that's okay, man. I'm cool. (*turns to leave*) I gotta get to class. (*exits*)

In English class, SHARI and AUDRA have taken seats in the back. MR. RICH is taking roll.

MR. RICH Shari and Audra, I almost counted you two absent. Would you please take your assigned seats? The rest of this film is important for you to watch. I'd rather you didn't sit in the back.

SHARI (*in a loud voice*) We're cool back here, Mr. Rich.

MR. RICH (*peers at her intently for a moment*) Well, I suppose it's okay for today. Just don't talk during the film, okay?

SHARI (*feeling dizzy*) You know we wouldn't do that, right Audra? (*laughs loudly*)

MR. RICH (*looks at her intently again*) Are you okay, Shari?

AUDRA (*covering for her*) She's okay, Mr. Rich. I think she's in love, or something. Just start the film, will you?

MR. RICH (*looking doubtfully at both of them*) Okay. (*Turns out the lights, starts the film, then sits down and bends over some papers on his desk.*)

SHARI (*to AUDRA in a loud whisper*) Audra! Audra! Go with me to the bathroom, will you? I don't feel so good.

AUDRA   Uh-oh. You look weird. (*glances toward MR. RICH who is looking down at papers on his desk*) Come on. He won't see us.

SHARI   Okay. I hope I can get out the door. I feel really weird. (*The two girls exit. Outside the door, SHARI stumbles toward a nearby bench and slumps down. AUDRA grabs her to keep her from falling.*)

AUDRA   Shari, sit up! What's the matter, girl! Come on, sit up! (*Looks into SHARI'S eyes.*) Oh, my God. Oh, my God! (*Looks around desperately for somebody to help. KARLTON is walking by with a pass to the office.*) Karlton, Karlton, come here and look at this. Look! Her eyes are rolled back in her head.

KARLTON (*steps over and looks in SHARI'S face*)   Oh, my God! She's overdosing. We've gotta get help. This looks bad. (*glances around wildly*) You stay here with her. I'll go get the principal.

AUDRA   Hey, no. We'll get in trouble. She'll get suspended.

Discussion

1. Did Paul mean to hurt Shari? Explain.
2. Why did he want to share his spiked drink with other students?
3. What could have been added to the orange soda that might have had such a serious effect on Shari?
4. Name all the bad things that could happen to Shari because of this situation.
5. Is Karlton right in wanting to get immediate help for Shari?
6. Should Audra tell who gave Shari the spiked drink?
7. If she doesn't tell, who might be hurt? If she does tell, who might be helped?
8. What is the best thing for Audra to do?
9. What would you do?

Doing wrong to belong

I Can Drink the Whole Thing

CHARACTERS
TROY, OLIVIA, KEN, LOUIS, PAM, POLICE OFFICER, FIRST PARAMEDIC, SECOND PARAMEDIC

Students are partying at KEN's house. His parents are on vacation. LOUIS, who is over 21, has brought cases of beer and hard liquor.

KEN   Hey, turn the music up just a little bit, will you, Troy? Not too much, or the neighbors will call the cops. And drink up, you guys.

PAM (*to Olivia*)   You didn't tell me these guys would drink so much. I hope they don't get stupid. I wanna dance, and drunk guys get so sloppy, you know what I mean?

OLIVIA   Oh, don't worry about it. They're cool. Just have a good time. Drink a little more yourself and you won't even notice.

PAM (*She frowns.*)   I just wanna dance. (*She looks toward the table, where the guys have gathered around, talking and drinking. She gestures toward them.*) I think they just wanna drink. (*She begins to dance by herself.*)

TROY (*looking admiringly at Pam*)   Nice. Very nice. (*He approaches her and begins to dance.*) How'd you learn to dance so well?

PAM (*looking at him and smiling*)   Oh, I think it runs in my family.

OLIVIA (*approaching them*)   Hey, aren't you guys drinking anything? (*She takes a long drink from her beer.*)

TROY (*not wanting to sound uncool*)   Hey, Olivia, we can keep up with the best of you. Don't get all fussed up. We gotta work off a little energy. (*They continue dancing.*)

LOUIS (*approaching them*)   I heard that. I take that as a challenge. Hey, Ken, Troy says he can keep up with the best of us. I don't think so.

KEN   What? So Troy thinks he can keep up with *me*? (*to TROY*) Troy? Troy! (*TROY keeps dancing.*) Hey, Troy! (*TROY finally looks at him and stands still.*)

TROY (*to PAM*)   Put me on hold a few minutes, will you? (*turning to KEN*) What's up, man? It better be good.

LOUIS (*approaching*)   Troy, Ken wants to propose a challenge. (*He is holding in either hand an unopened bottle of vodka.*)

OLIVIA   Uh-oh. This'll be good.

KEN   Come on, man. Let's see what kinda stuff you're made of. I challenge you to see which of us can chug-a-lug the most in fifteen seconds. What do you say? (*He turns to OLIVIA.*) He may be a good dancer, but I can out drink him any day.

TROY (*Fidgets and does not want to accept the challenge.*)   Man, I'd rather dance with this beautiful woman. But you give me no choice.

PAM   Hey, Troy, you don't have to do this. (*more emphatically*) Hey, it's dangerous.

OLIVIA   Oh, relax, Pam. I've seen this before. It's no big deal. Guys just wanna have fun.

PAM   Honestly, you guys are so immature. (*She laughs.*) Well, I don't want to watch. I'm going to go freshen up. But you better not mess up my dance partner. (*exits*)

LOUIS (*opening the bottles and handing one to KEN and TROY*)   Okay. Get ready. I'll let you know when to start. (*He checks his watch a moment. KEN and TROY each plant their feet firmly and watch LOUIS's face.*) Okay, go! (*KEN and TROY lean back slightly and begin to chug-a-lug. TROY drinks slower than KEN.*)

OLIVIA (*shouting*)   Come on, Troy! You can do better than that!

LOUIS (*counting*)   Five, four, three, two, one. Okay. Stop. Give me the bottles. (*They stop, steady themselves, and hand LOUIS the bottles. LOUIS takes them to the table and sets them down. KEN's is nearly half-empty, while TROY's is down much less.*)

KEN (*grinning toward TROY*)   Hey, man. I beat you fair and square. You're gonna have to practice.

PAM (*enters*)   You guys done now, I hope?

OLIVIA   Yeah. Hey, you missed the whole thing. I don't think your dancer buddy was serious. Ken kicked his butt.

PAM (*a bit snippy*)   Well, maybe that'll mean Troy'll be able to dance some more instead of sprawl around with a stupid grin on his face. No offense meant, Ken.

KEN   Hey, no offense taken. A man is a man, and I'm the man here. I won fair and square.

OLIVIA   So what's the prize?

TROY (*steadying himself*)   Hey, I won, because I still get to dance with Pam. (*He starts towards her.*)

KEN   Well, I'm tired now after my stunning victory, so I think I'll sit this one out. Wanna come over here and praise the winner, Olivia? (*He flops down on the couch.*)

OLIVIA (*looking intently at him*)   No, you look a little pale. I think you need to cool it a while. Maybe I can get Louis to dance with me.

LOUIS (*pouring himself another drink*)   Well, okay, but I'm not very good. Especially since my rule is I can't set down my drink. (*He laughs.*)

While the four are dancing, KEN leans his head back on the couch and shuts his eyes. After a while, he slumps to the side and begins to drool. Soon, TROY is feeling dizzy.

TROY   Hey, Pam. I'm not feeling so good. Excuse me a minute, will you? (*He exits unsteadily.*)

PAM (*Watches him a moment, then turns toward the couch.*)   Well, I think I'll take it easy a few minutes. These shoes are too tight. (*Heads for the couch, sits down, slips off her shoes, and rubs her feet. Then she turns toward KEN.*) Ken? Hey, what's the matter? (*looks toward the others uneasily*) Hey, you guys, I think he passed out.

LOUIS   Well, I need another drink. Don't worry about it, Pam. He'll sleep it off. I've seen him do this before. (*OLIVIA and LOUIS head for the drink table.*)

PAM (*Looks doubtfully after them, then turns again to KEN.*)   Ken? (*louder*) Ken? (*Reaches over and pushes him back up straight, but he slumps over again; to herself.*) This isn't right. (*Stands up over him, grabs him by the shoulders, and shakes him gently.*) Ken? Ken, wake up! (*His head flops backwards and his eyes are partially open, but she sees only the whites of his eyes. She turns towards the others and sounds panicked.*) You guys, come here and look at him! Something's really wrong. He's not right. This is not just sleeping.

LOUIS   All right. All right. (*Approaches and bends over Ken, peering into his face. He pushes the lid of one eye back and sees that his eyes are rolled back.*) Hmmm! He hasn't done this before. Ken? Hey, man. (*begins to shake him*)

OLIVIA (*approaching and bending over KEN*)   Oh, my God. Oh, my God! I don't like this one bit. It doesn't look like he's breathing.

PAM   We gotta do something. He looks like he could die. We better call the paramedics.

LOUIS   Hold up, hold up! I could get in real trouble. I'm the only one here over 21. (*Looks again at KEN, then faces the two girls.*) Tell you what. Let me get out of here, then you call.

OLIVIA   This sucks! Okay, get out of here. Man, this sucks. And we're in Ken's house. This'll really look bad. We're gonna get in bad trouble.

LOUIS   Well, you guys can handle it. You won't get in as much trouble as I would. I'm outta here. (*exits*)

PAM   Whatta man! Well, I'm gonna call. (*Goes to a phone on a nearby coffee table and dials 911.*)

TROY (*entering*)   Man, I'm never gonna do that again. I've been throwing up. (*seeing PAM on the phone*) What's up?

OLIVIA   She's calling 911. Ken's not looking so good.

Soon sirens approach the house. A police officer enters first, bends over KEN, then looks at the three.

OFFICER   You wanna tell me what's been going on here?

OLIVIA   We were just having a little party.

OFFICER (*Takes out his notepad. The siren of the ambulance can be heard nearing the house.*) Do you girls live here?

PAM (*gesturing toward KEN*)   No. This is his place.

OFFICER   So what adults are present here? How old is he? (*gesturing toward KEN*)

OLIVIA   I think he's seventeen. We had his birthday party here last summer.

OFFICER   Just seventeen, huh. That's not good. You kids have been drinking, haven't you? (*not waiting for an answer*) How about him? Where are his parents?

OLIVIA   Ken said they were on a vacation. I don't know where they went.

OFFICER   So how much did he drink?

PAM   They had a chug-a-lug contest. I couldn't stand to watch so I left the room. I don't really know, but it was a lot.

TROY   I'll tell you, sir. It was almost half a bottle of vodka.

Two paramedics enter and hurry over to Ken.

FIRST PARAMEDIC (*to OFFICER*)   What's the situation here, sir?

OFFICER   It looks like an alcohol overdose. Could be life-threatening. He's got to be treated. Get him out of here right now. Get out of the way, you kids.

SECOND PARAMEDIC   We'd better hurry. (*They hurry out to get the stretcher.*)

OFFICER   You kids pay good attention, now. Your friend here is in real trouble. Too much alcohol at once can make a heart quit. (*PARAMEDICS enter with the stretcher.*)

FIRST PARAMEDIC   Looks like a close one. This one's gonna get Code 3.

SECOND PARAMEDIC (*rises from listening to his heart*)   Pulse very weak. Respiration shallow. (*PARAMEDICS load up KEN, and exit, wheeling him out. A siren is heard fading away into the night.*)

OLIVIA   Well, I gotta go now. My folks are expecting me home. (*edges toward the door*)

OFFICER   Wait a minute, young lady. That's not how it works. Sit down. (*OLIVIA, PAM, and TROY sit down stiffly and stare with worried faces at him.*) You wanna tell me where all this liquor came from?

Discussion

1. Why do you think Ken invited friends over while his parents are gone?
2. Why do you think Pam, Olivia, and Troy came to Ken's party?
3. Why do you think Louis brought the liquor for them besides the fact that he could legally buy it? What laws has he broken?
4. Why did Ken pass out? What has actually happened to his body? How dangerous is this?
5. What punishment could Ken get, if he lives? What punishment could Troy, Pam, and Olivia get? What punishment could Louis get?
6. Should the law hold Ken's parents responsible for what happened while they were gone?
7. Are the laws fair that don't allow underage kids to drink? Explain.
8. How could the kids have had a good time without using alcohol or other drugs?

Can I Borrow Your Homework?

CHARACTERS

MELVIN, BARBARA, MR. BENZA, MISS LAYNE (substitute teacher)

MISS LAYNE, the substitute teacher, has taken roll and written the day's assignment on the board. The students are supposed to finish an introduction to a notebook they have been working on for four weeks. It contains a daily observation journal of their science experiments.

BARBARA (*whispering*)   Melvin! Hey, Melvin.

MELVIN (*looking up from his notebook*)   Yeah?

BARBARA   Hey, can I ask you a favor?

MELVIN (*frowns*)   I guess so. What is it?

BARBARA   You got your notebook done?

MELVIN   Almost. I'm just finishing my final copy of the introduction. How's yours coming?

BARBARA   Well, I'm having a hard time. I'm not sure what Benza wants. I sure could use some help.

MELVIN   Like what? We've been working on these for four weeks. You should be about done.

BARBARA (*Smiles flirtatiously at him.*)   Well, that's just the problem. I just couldn't get into it, you know what I mean?

MELVIN   Uh-oh. You're almost out of time. What are you going to do about it?

BARBARA   Well, that's what I wanted to ask you.

MELVIN   I think I get your drift. You want to look at mine?

BARBARA   Well, yeah. Do you suppose I could borrow it overnight? I promise I'll bring it back to you tomorrow. You don't want to hand yours in to a substitute, do you? You know, you can tell Benza that you wanted to give it to him personally. You're such a good student, he'll buy it.

MELVIN   Well, I could let you look at it just if you want to see how I've got it organized, but I wouldn't want to let you take it home. One other time I did that, the guy didn't show back up at school for a week and I got marked down because my work was late. I learned that lesson.

BARBARA   Shoot. I'm really in a mess. I just want to look. Then I can be sure I know what to do and get it all done this weekend.

MELVIN   Well, I've got to go down to the gym for a few minutes to help Coach get his computer straightened out, so I'll leave the notebook on my desk. You look at it while I'm gone. Okay? Maybe you could get a pass to the office and make yourself a copy. Just change it a bunch when you make yours so nobody will know.

BARBARA   Cool. Uh-oh, the sub is glaring at us.

MISS LAYNE   Students, please no talking. You've got work to do.

MELVIN   Sorry, Miss Layne. (*Rises and heads toward the desk where MISS LAYNE is sitting.*) Excuse me, Miss Layne, but I've got to go down to the gym. Coach asked me if I could come down today and help him with his computer. He gave me this note. (*Hands her a note from COACH.*) I'll only be gone about fifteen minutes.

MISS LAYNE (*Reads the note, then smiles up at him.*)   Sure, okay. Your name is Melvin?

MELVIN (*nods*)   Thanks. I'll be back.

As soon as MELVIN steps out, BARBARA takes MELVIN's notebook from his desk. After she has paged through it, she closes it and carries it up to MISS LAYNE.

BARBARA   Teacher, can I have a pass to the office? I've gotta call my mother to see what time she's going to pick me up for the dentist.

MISS LAYNE (*frowning*)   I suppose so. (*Writes a pass. BARBARA exits carrying MELVIN's notebook.*)

BARBARA (*Enters office. Approaches the secretary.*)   Ma'am, the sub down there for Mr. Benza, she asked me to make some copies for her, okay? (*Secretary nods, so BARBARA begins to photocopy all the pages of the notebook. When she finishes, she returns to the class and places the notebook on MELVIN's desk before he gets back.*)

Later, when MR. BENZA is checking the notebooks, he notices that BARBARA's is almost identical to MELVIN's. He asks both students to come in after class.

MR. BENZA   We've got a problem here. These two notebooks are almost identical. I know you both didn't do the exact same experiment and make the exact same observations. Do you want to explain this to me?

MELVIN   Really, Mr. Benza. That can't be possible. (*Begins to fidget.*)

MR. BENZA   Well, you know my policy on cheating. This looks bad. Somebody copied somebody's work. This means I can't give either one of you credit. I'm really disappointed. (*Turns to BARBARA.*) So what do you have to say about this?

BARBARA (*shrugs*)   Hey, I don't know. I can't believe you're accusing me of cheating.

MR. BENZA   I asked both of you for an explanation, but it doesn't look like I'm going to get it. Melvin, you've been good about getting your work in on time, and I know you're concerned about your GPA, but I have to do what I have to do. You know we have a zero tolerance about cheating.

MELVIN   Mr. Benza, please. All I did was tell her she could see how I did my notebook. I don't know how she copied what I did.

BARBARA (*getting snotty*)   Hey, maybe *you* copied what I did.

MR. BENZA   And that is why I must disqualify both of these notebooks.

BARBARA   Well, this class sucks anyway. (*Stalks out of the room.*)

MELVIN   Honestly, Mr. Benza, I don't know how this happened. Is there any way I can make this up? Can I do another whole project or something? We still have a week left. I would work my hind end off.

MR. BENZA (*thinking a moment*)   Well, I think maybe we could work out something like that. Can you have it done by next Friday? (*MELVIN nods.*) And tell Barbara she can do the same thing. Okay?

Later, BARBARA approaches MELVIN in hallway.

BARBARA   Hey, Melvin. (*He turns and faces her.*) Hey, I'm really sorry about that. I just don't have time for all this boring stuff. I think I'm going to flunk anyway.

MELVIN   You put me in a bind. Thank goodness he's letting us redo the work. I'm really going to have to hit the books this week to get ready for the test Friday. I gotta be going. (*Turns and walks away.*)

BARBARA (*calling after him*)   I really am sorry.

Discussion

1. Why would Melvin be willing to let Barbara copy his work?
2. Should Melvin be punished for letting Barbara copy his work?
3. Who would be hurt if Barbara continues to cheat?
4. How could Melvin have better handled the situation?
5. Should Mr. Benza have given them a chance to do their work over?
6. If Barbara asked you for a look at your work, what would you do?

They're Not Home; Let's Sneak In

CHARACTERS
ALLEN, CONNIE, RALPH, SERENA, POLICE OFFICER, MRS. THOMAS (neighbor)

An old couple has been on vacation for a week. MRS. THOMAS has been watching their house for them. ALLEN, CONNIE, RALPH, and SERENA pass by on their way home from school.

CONNIE   That old lady hasn't been out in her yard lately. She always stares at me when I walk by, like she doesn't like how I look, ya know what I mean?

SERENA   Boy, do I! I hate when old people glare at us because we look different. As if they were perfect when they were young.

RALPH   Yeah, the old man got in a fuss at me last week when I dropped a gum wrapper on the sidewalk. Shoot, he doesn't own the sidewalk.

ALLEN   Well, he thinks he does. Somebody needs to teach them a lesson.

CONNIE (*They pause in front of the house.*)   Like what? They haven't really hurt me, or anything. You know, we could walk on the other side of the street.

SERENA   What? Just because of them? Heck no, we've got rights. So Allen, you got any ideas what kind of lesson we could teach them?

ALLEN   Maybe. Some friends of mine got some cool stuff out of a house over a few blocks. Those people were stupid. They didn't even lock the back door.

RALPH   You mean they stole stuff? I don't know, man. You can get in real trouble for that.

ALLEN   Not if you don't get caught.

CONNIE   What are you guys thinking? I don't like where this conversation is going.

SERENA   Oh, grow up, Connie. The world's a tough place. Survival of the fittest, you know.

MRS. THOMAS (*stepping out on her porch and addressing the kids*)   Listen, you kids, you move on now. Those folks are out of town a while. You shouldn't be loitering around here. Go fool around in your own neighborhood.

SERENA (*snottily*)   Shove it, lady. You can't tell us what to do.

MRS. THOMAS (*to herself*)   Punks! This neighborhood's going down the drain. (*She enters her house, closes the door, and then watches the kids from behind her curtains.*)

ALLEN (*to RALPH and CONNIE*)   See what I mean? You wanna take crap offa people or not? I don't. I say we give these old nosy busybodies a lesson in minding their own business. You know, shake up their world a little.

RALPH   Man, what do you have in mind? Like egg their house or something? My mom's still wondering what happened to her missing eggs from the last time when we drove around in your dad's car and egged parked cars. I told her I made a bunch of fried-egg sandwiches. She bought that story, but I'd never get away with it again. So who's got some eggs?

ALLEN   No, I got a more advanced idea.

SERENA   I think I know what he means. (*turning to ALLEN*) You mean going in their house and making ourselves at home a while, don't you? Like last time.

CONNIE (*becoming alarmed*)   What last time?

SERENA   Hey, I don't tell you everything. It was really fun. We went into this empty house and did some art on the walls, had a little sorta party. You get my drift?

RALPH   You didn't get caught?

ALLEN   No, of course not. But we did see cop cars over there after the owner discovered our little mischief. If we decide to go in this house, we'll have to do it after dark and keep quiet. Maybe they left some food or booze or something I could give my dad for a birthday present.

SERENA   Hey, I'm on. When are we gonna do this?

ALLEN   We better do it tonight. We don't know when they're coming back. We don't want to be caught in there.

SERENA   Yeah, that would suck. (*turning toward RALPH and CONNIE*) You guys down for this?

CONNIE (*looking down and shuffling her feet*)   I don't know about this.

RALPH   I don't think it's my style. You guys go ahead. Just pretend I'm along, okay?

A car drives by, so they continue on down the street and stop in front of a market.

ALLEN   I knew it! I knew you were a lightweight. I don't blame Connie for being a wuss because she's a girl, but you, man. I thought you weren't such a chicken!

SERENA   Some got it, some don't. (*looks at her watch*) Well, I got things to do. (*to CONNIE*) But don't ever complain to me again about how the old lady looks at you. You *better* walk on the other side of the street from now on.

ALLEN   Hey, it's no big deal. We won't really hurt anything. How'll you know what you're missing if you don't give it a try? Every kid needs some adventures to tell their grandchildren about. Your chance is going, going, going . . .

RALPH   Well, okay. I'm no lightweight. I guess I could try it once. I don't like the old goats much myself. (*to CONNIE*) Come on, girl. If you don't have fun, you can blame me.

CONNIE (*still very uneasy*)   You're twisting my arm, Ralph. (*pause*) But I guess I don't wanna be a wet blanket. Just this once, though. Maybe the old geezers will learn a lesson.

ALLEN   Okay, cool. So here's the plan. (*They gather into a huddle.*) Tonight, about 8:30, let's all meet at Serena's house. (*to CONNIE*) Can you tell your mom you're going over there to study for a test for a while, or something?

CONNIE   Yeah, I think that'll work.

ALLEN   So then we'll go around the block and go up the alley to their back yard. I'll go find a way in while Ralph keeps watch. You girls can hide behind some bushes until I give you the signal. Okay?

SERENA   Sounds good so far. Are you guys on, for sure?

CONNIE   Yeah.

RALPH   Yep. See ya at 8:30 then.

Their plan is in motion. ALLEN breaks a window in the back door. They enter the house and are groping around from the dim light of the street lamp through the windows. But the neighbor, MRS. THOMAS, spots them going in when she looks out her window to see why her dog is barking. She calls the police.

RALPH   Hey, here's the kitchen. Let's see if they left any munchies in the fridge. (*Opens the door of the refrigerator. The light illumines his face. He spots some cans of beer and a block of cheese. He takes them out and sits down on the floor.*) Cool.

ALLEN   Quiet, you guys. I'm going in the bedroom and see if they have any jewels. They won't miss one or two little things. (*SERENA takes out a small flashlight and tags along with him. CONNIE is close behind.*)

SERENA   Yeah, I love rings. (*She finds the jewel box on top of the dresser and stuffs her pocket with rings.*)

CONNIE (*watching ALLEN yank open drawers and dump the contents on the floor*)   I'm scared, you guys. Let's get out of here.

ALLEN (*Finds a gold watch.*)   Aha! My dad will like this. (*Stuffs it in his pocket.*)

RALPH (*calling softly to CONNIE*)   Connie, come in here. I hate to eat alone. (*She turns to join him in the kitchen.*)

A police car pulls up out front with its lights off. An OFFICER gets out with his flashlight and begins to shine it around the yard and front porch. RALPH sees the light shine across the kitchen wall.

RALPH (*scrambling to his feet, then ducking down*)   Uh-oh. Somebody's coming!

OFFICER (*Calls out.*)   Okay, I know you're in there. Come on out here now with your hands up.

ALLEN (*to SERENA*) Uh-oh. Shhh. He doesn't know we're still here. Come on, let's go out this bedroom window.

The OFFICER hears their voices. He comes into the house and finds CONNIE and RALPH trying to hide in the entry hall.

OFFICER   Okay, you two. Freeze right there. (*Shines his flashlight into their faces, then speaks into his hand-held radio.*) I need back up. I've found two inside, but I heard more voices. Send them up the alley in case someone tries to get out. (*to RALPH and CONNIE*) Just what do you two think you're doing in here? Who else is in the house?

CONNIE   Oh, God. We didn't mean any harm. You won't tell my mom, will you? She thinks I went to study at Serena's.

OFFICER   So is Serena in here, too?

RALPH (*trying to cover for SERENA and ALLEN*)   No. It's just the two of us. We were hungry.

OFFICER   Listen, young man, lying to a police office is another offense, besides breaking and entering.

MRS. THOMAS (*yelling from outside the house*)   There they go! There they go! Those punks!

Another squad car pulls up in the alley and this officer apprehends SERENA and ALLEN. They are sitting dejectedly on the ground with their hands cuffed behind them. The OFFICER in the house comes out behind CONNIE and RALPH. MRS. THOMAS is watching over her fence.

OFFICER   So, are these the ones you saw, ma'am.

MRS. THOMAS (*nodding*)   That's them, the ones I always see loitering around the street.

Discussion

1. Why do you think Allen and Serena have broken into a house before? Is this a good way to get respect? Explain.
2. Why do Connie and Ralph decide to go along with Allen and Serena?
3. What is likely to happen to the kids now that the officers have them in custody?
4. Which ones of the four are likely to get the most serious punishment? Why?
5. Is there a better way the elderly homeowners could have treated the kids as they walked up the street? Are they to blame for what happened to the kids in any way?
6. How do you feel about how Mrs. Thomas handled the situation?
7. How could the kids have better handled what they considered the disrespectful behavior of the old people?

Hold This Pipe for Me

CHARACTERS

JOEY, GERALD, WANDA, COLLEEN, MR. HILL (teacher), POLICE OFFICER

When WANDA comes back into math class from the restroom, she warns others of a search taking place in another classroom down the corridor.

WANDA (*whispering to JOEY*)   Joey? Joey! They're doing a search!

JOEY   Where? School police?

WANDA   Yeah. I just saw them down by the B-Wing. It looks serious.

MR. HILL   Quiet back there, please. If a search is taking place, I can't let any more kids have passes to the restrooms or their lockers. Sorry. If the officers come in here, just do what they say. They'll probably only search some of you at random.

GERALD (*raising his hand*)   What are they looking for, Mr. Hill?

MR. HILL   Oh, they probably got a tip that some kind of contraband was on campus. You know, maybe drugs or weapons. They're just doing their jobs.

GERALD   Thanks. (*to himself*) Boy, I'm glad I don't have anything to worry about.

COLLEEN (*to GERALD*)   Gerald, do me a favor, will you? (*Smiles flirtatiously at him.*)

GERALD (*blushing, and flattered at the attention*)   Sure. What is it?

COLLEEN   Well, I've got to go somewhere after third period. Would you take this make-up case I borrowed from LeeAnn and give it to her when you see her? You've got her in fourth period history, don't you? I promised her I'd give it back to her today. You can just stick it in your backpack until then. Would you do that for me?

MR. HILL   Colleen, please.

GERALD (*whispering*)   Okay. No sweat. Consider it done.

COLLEEN (*smiling sweetly at him*)   Thanks. You don't know how much I appreciate that.

WANDA (*to JOEY*)   Hey, Colleen gave Gerald some make-up. Do you suppose he's a cross-dresser? (*Snickers at her snide comment.*)

JOEY   Really? Well, maybe. I know he's not much of an athlete, at least what I've seen. That's weird though.

The class quiets down and resumes studying. Suddenly, the door bursts open and in steps a police officer and his assistant.

JOEY   Uh-oh. They're here.

WANDA   See. I told you. Something's up around here.

OFFICER   Okay, students. This is a formal search, conducted according to the Education Code. According to law, we have the right to search you, your clothing, your backpacks, and any place in the room. When I give you instruction, you will step outside the door to be searched by our metal detector. You will leave all purses, books, and possessions where they are.

JOEY (*trying to be humorous*)   Gee, I'm glad I left my AK-47 home today. (*A few students giggle nervously.*)

OFFICER   Young man, we don't joke about this. I'm going to treat you like you meant that. Mr. Hill, would you accompany this young man to the holding area? We're going to have to investigate this matter thoroughly. Any other confessions anyone would like to make? (*MR. HILL and JOEY exit.*)

COLLEEN   Well, I just want you to know me and my friends really appreciate that you're doing this. There's some real slime in this school.

WANDA (*to herself*)   Have you looked in the mirror lately?

OFFICER   What's that, young lady?

WANDA   Oh, nothing. Sorry, sir. Just so everyone knows, when I go out that door, my purse contains fifteen dollars and some change. Nobody but the officer better touch it.

GERALD (*trying to be sympathetic*)   Sounds like you've had some hard lessons.

WANDA (*smiling at him*)   Yeah, I've already learned that one.

OFFICER   No more talking now. I'd like this row to go. (*Indicates the row Gerald and Wanda are sitting in. They exit.*)

MR. HILL (*enters*)   Well, Joey's pretty upset. I bet he'll never make a joke like that again. (*Looks around at the few remaining solemn faces.*) You want me to take anymore of them down?

OFFICER   Not yet. I hope that's the worst problem we find. (*Gestures to the last row where Colleen is sitting.*) Okay, you can go out.

COLLEEN   Gosh, these things are such a waste of time.

OFFICER   I hope so, young lady. Will you tell my assistant to keep everyone out there in a group until I let them know it's okay to come back in? (*COLLEEN's row exits. He begins to search the room systematically: the wastebasket, the bookshelves, under cabinets, and finally, the purses, backpacks, books, and possessions the kids have left around their desks. When he gets to GERALD's backpack, he takes out the make-up case COLLEEN asked him to give to LeeAnn later. The officer looks at it, shakes his head, and opens it. Inside is a book of matches, several small plastic bags containing methamphetamine crystals, and a small pipe.*)

MR. HILL   Bingo! Which purse did you find that in?

OFFICER   No purse. A guy's backpack. This one. (*Holds up GERALD's backpack.*) Funny a guy would keep his works in a girl's make-up bag. But what's really bad is that there's enough stuff in here to indicate that we have a dealer. This kid's in real trouble.

MR. HILL   That looks like Gerald's pack. He's a good student. That doesn't seem like him. He's kind of quiet. Hasn't seemed to make many friends around here, though. I sure hate to see that. What do you want me to do now?

OFFICER   Call him in here, will you?

MR. HILL   Sure. (*Steps to door and calls GERALD inside.*) Gerald, the officer needs to speak to you.

GERALD   Really? What for? Have I been a witness to a crime or something? (*Sees the OFFICER standing over his open backpack and the make-up case open on the desk. He sees the drug paraphernalia.*) Oh, no.

OFFICER   "Oh no" is right, Son. This is big trouble. Possession of paraphernalia, and enough meth in here to show intent to sell. The last is cause for expulsion.

GERALD   But that's not my stuff. I was just holding it for a girl to give to her friend for her in fourth period. I don't use drugs. I thought it was just make-up. You know, girl stuff. She asked me to do her a favor.

OFFICER   Well, Son, sorry I can't accept your story right now. People who break the law seldom tell the truth when they're caught. And you're caught. (*turning to MR. HILL*) Mr. Hill, would you accompany this young man down to the holding area? I'll be along in a few minutes as soon as I've finished searching this last row.

MR. HILL   Yes, but this upsets me. (*to GERALD*) I can't believe you'd get involved in this, Gerald. Let's go. (*They exit.*)

GERALD (*seated beside MR. HILL in the holding area*)   But I didn't know she was giving me anything illegal. Honest. Or I wouldn't have taken it. You've gotta believe me.

MR. HILL   I'd like to Gerald, but that's not how the system works. Can you think of anyone who might have seen the girl give you the case? By the way, what girl was it?

GERALD   I'd rather not say, Mr. Hill.

MR. HILL   Well, if you *are* telling the truth, the only way you can get your name cleared even a little is if you give us her name and we can find corroborating witnesses.

GERALD   Looks like I'll be in trouble no matter what I do.

MR. HILL   Looks like it.

In the holding area, GERALD sits disconsolately, head down. He has given COLLEEN's name to the officer and suggested that WANDA may have witnessed COLLEEN giving him the make-up case. In the principal's office, the officer is questioning WANDA.

OFFICER   So, your name is Wanda, right? (*She nods.*) Okay, Gerald said maybe you saw Colleen hand him a make-up case in math this morning? Is that right?

WANDA (*fidgeting and looking away*)   Do I have to answer?

OFFICER   Yes, you do. It's much better to tell the truth than it is to try to protect a drug dealer.

WANDA (*nodding her head in agreement*)   I guess.

OFFICER   Well?

WANDA   Okay, yes, I saw her hand it to him. It was after I came in and blabbed that I saw a search going on. I wondered what in the heck she was talking to him for. He's not her type. She hangs out with some real loose kids, know what I mean. And Gerald, he's just a bookworm, real quiet, shy, but nice. Is that what you need to know?

OFFICER   Yes, that's helpful. Is there anything else you could tell me to help me get to the bottom of this?

WANDA   Just that you don't have to let Colleen know I'm the one who told you, do you? She's into some real dirty business, I hear. I don't want any trouble.

OFFICER   Well, not if she admits the stuff was hers. We'll see. Okay, thank you very much. You can go back to class. (*WANDA exits.*)

COLLEEN is called in for questioning next. GERALD watches nervously from the holding area.

OFFICER   So, Colleen, is it? (*She nods.*) Is this your make-up case? (*He pushes it towards her across the desk.*)

COLLEEN   Heck, no. I don't have any stupid stuff like that. Who told you that! Some creep around here is trying to get me in trouble.

OFFICER   Well, we have two witnesses that say you gave this to a boy in math class to give to one of your friends later, after you heard a search was going on.

COLLEEN   Gerald? Did Gerald say that? That punk!

OFFICER   How do you know it was Gerald?

COLLEEN (*Her face goes red.*)   Well, I didn't give him anything. What a liar! Who's the other witness? You don't have any proof of anything. I hate this place!

Discussion

1. Why do you think Gerald took the make-up case from Colleen to give to LeeAnn?
2. Why do you think Colleen chose Gerald as the one to pass off her drug supply to?
3. Why do you think schools conduct such searches? What is bad about them? What is good about them? Are they necessary?
4. Did Wanda do the right thing in naming Colleen as the owner of the make-up case?
5. Gerald was in possession of drugs and paraphernalia in a school. What punishment do you think is appropriate for him?
6. Why do you think Colleen's possession-with-intent-to-sell offense was so serious? Who all was she hurting?
7. How can Gerald avoid problems like this in the future?

The Store Will Never Miss This

CHARACTERS
ADRIANA, COLLETTE, CHARLIE, JEWELRY CLERK, STORE SECURITY OFFICER

ADRIANA, COLLETTE, and CHARLIE are strolling through the mall. CHARLIE wants the girls to help him find a bracelet for his girlfriend, Megan.

ADRIANA   So, Charlie, are you going to spring for real gold? Megan's got expensive taste, you know.

COLLETTE   Yeah, Charlie. Her last boyfriend drove a BMW. Of course, his daddy gave it to him. But, be careful around her.

CHARLIE   I hear you guys. But her birthday's a big deal. Her parents are throwing a party and barbeque, and I've got to have something nice. Trouble is, I've only got fourteen dollars.

ADRIANA   Well, that won't even buy her a bottle of so-so perfume. You could get her a pretty fancy card though.

CHARLIE   Big deal. That won't cut it. I probably shouldn't even try to be with her when I'm not really in her class. But she calls me up all the time and wants me to come over. And I do think she's hot. In spite of what I hear people saying about her, she's really nice. Shoot, why am I telling you guys my personal business. You're not "Dear Abby."

COLLETTE   Hey, that's what friends do. Listen to each other. We have been friends since third grade.

CHARLIE   True, but my dad wonders why I don't hang out more with the jocks.

ADRIANA   Well, did you tell him that jocks can't help you pick out a bracelet for your girl? So don't start getting ashamed of us. (*They enter a department store and approach the jewelry counter.*) Here, Charlie. Here are some nice bracelets. Look, they start at only thirty dollars. That's on sale, too.

COLLETTE   But they're so skimpy. Oh, look, here's one for sixty-five dollars. I bet Megan would like that. I know I would.

CHARLIE   Well, fourteen dollars is a long way from sixty-five, and then you've got to add tax. Sorry, no way. (*pause*) Maybe I'll tell her I can't come to her party. Heck, I'll never be able to keep up with what she's used to.

ADRIANA   Now Charlie, let's don't give up so fast. You say you need a nice gift. And a gold bracelet is really a nice gift. And here is one for sixty-five, and it would be a nice gift, so we better figure out how to get this one. I've got an idea how we can help you out, Charlie, but you'll owe us big time.

CHARLIE   Really, you mean you'll let me borrow the money? Where did you get that kind of money, anyway?

ADRIANA   Never mind. Listen, Charlie, here's little poem for you. "If you shop, and you lift, just consider it a gift." Get it? Just go along with the program, okay? Be cool, now.

CHARLIE   Hey, wait. I don't know about this. (*Squirms around but stays with them.*)

CLERK (*approaching*)   Sorry I kept you waiting. May I help you?

COLLETTE   Yes, we'd like to look at some of these bracelets.

CLERK (*Bends to unlock glass case.*)   Which one did you want to see?

ADRIANA (*pointing at a row of bracelets*)   Uh, the last three there. We should compare two or three of them, don't you think, Charlie?

CHARLIE   I guess so. I really don't know what I'm looking for.

CLERK (*laying the three bracelets out on a black velvet cloth*)   These are all very nice. They're 14 karat. Nice lobster claw clasps. Is this for a gift?

CHARLIE   Yeah, that's what I was hoping. But I don't know what girls like, so I brought along some experts. (*Laughs nervously.*)

ADRIANA (*stepping several feet down the counter and pointing at some silver bracelets*)   Uh, ma-am, could we also look at some of these?

CLERK   Surely. (*Steps down to the silver bracelets.*)

COLLETTE (*While the CLERK bends down to unlock the other case, she slips the sixty-five dollar bracelet off the counter into the pocket of her jacket, then grabs a cheap gold-plated bracelet off a revolving counter rack and lays it on the velvet in place of the gold bracelet.*)   Let's check those out, Charlie.

CHARLIE (*Has seen what COLLETTE did but doesn't know what to do about it.*)   Yeah, okay. (*The two step down to the silver bracelets.*)

ADRIANA   What do you think about these, Charlie? Or would you rather think about it a while, and you can come back later?

COLLETTE (*nodding knowingly at ADRIANA*)   Yeah, he probably better think about it.

CHARLIE   I guess so. We'd better go. (*The three start for the entrance to the store, but a STORE SECURITY OFFICER has been watching them carefully. He approaches them once they've stepped outside.*)

OFFICER   Hold up, you three. Just a minute. (*Steps in front of them and blocks their way.*)

ADRIANA (*innocently*)   What's the matter, sir? We gotta get home.

COLLETTE   Hey, what are you hassling us for? We didn't do anything. Get out of our way!

CHARLIE   Oh, God. (*under his breath*) What did I get myself into?

OFFICER   I need you to come with me into the security office. Come right now. If you're innocent, it will just take a couple of minutes.

ADRIANA   Innocent? Of doing what? Are you accusing us of something? I certainly am no thief. You don't have the right to hassle us just because we're kids.

OFFICER   You can come quietly without making a big fuss. I've already called for backup. Or you can be embarrassed right here in front of all the other customers.

Two other store security officers approach, and the three kids exit with them to the store security office. The three are searched. An officer finds the bracelet in COLLETTE's pocket.

OFFICER   Now we need you to give us your names and phone numbers. We'll check with our computer system to see if any of you have any records of prior criminal conduct. We'll contact your parents to let them know what's happening. (*Picks up a clipboard and pen to begin recording information.*) Who wants to start and get this over with?

ADRIANA   You didn't find anything on me. I want out of here. You can't hold me. I'm just a minor. You have no evidence against me.

COLLETTE   Great. What a fine friend you are!

OFFICER   Be quiet, you two. Since you have no manners, we'll start with the young man. What's your name?

ADRIANA   You don't have to tell him anything, Charlie.

OFFICER (*to ADRIANA*)   Next, I'll cuff you. Not another word! (*ADRIANA scowls and looks at the floor.*) Now, Charlie, what's your last name?

Soon, all three have given their names. Another security officer has checked with the computer. ADRIANA and COLLETTE have been apprehended before, but CHARLIE has a clean record.

OFFICER   Okay, ladies. We're not going to cut you any slack this time. We've called the P.D. and they'll be here in a few minutes to take you downtown. (*The girls just hang their heads.*) Charlie, since you have no previous record, we've called your father and he'll be here to pick you up shortly. He's not in a very good mood. Let this be a warning to you. If you considered these girls to be your friends, you'd best reconsider. True friends want what's best for you. This sure isn't it.

CHARLIE (*looking at the girls who won't give him eye contact*)   Wow. I guess you're right. (*shaking his head*) Man, my dad's going to kill me. I'll be on restriction the rest of my life. I should have known better.

Discussion

1. How could Charlie have honored Megan's birthday in spite of the fact he didn't have much money?
2. If Megan only wanted to be with him for expensive gifts he might give her, would she be a true friend? Explain.
3. Why do Adriana and Collette want to shoplift to help Charlie out?
4. What is wrong with shoplifting anyway? Explain.
5. In the future, what should Charlie do about his friendship with Adriana and Collette?
6. What is an important lesson Charlie can learn from this experience? Explain.
7. If you were with friends who wanted to shoplift, what would you do?

Everybody Ditches Sometime, Don't They?

CHARACTERS
JAMES, LENNIE, ARMANDO, CECELIA, PATRICIA, NEIGHBOR LADY, POLICE DISPATCHER, POLICE OFFICER

It is lunchtime and a group of students are gathered around a table.

JAMES   Man, only five more minutes. I can't stand my next class. It's so boring. It's time for a change.

LENNIE   Hey, I agree. That lady talks way too much. I just wanna draw, you know, and she walks around all the time harping away about keeping on task. You wanna split? My folks are both at work. We could go hang out a little.

ARMANDO   Sounds cool. Can Cecelia and I come along? We never get any time to ourselves. I'd like to listen to some music and … you know.

CECELIA   Armando, shut up. Gentlemen don't blab.

LENNIE   Hey, Cecelia's always welcome. You got any friends, you know, of the feminine persuasion that might come along? We could really get down!

JAMES   Now I'm really getting interested.

CECELIA   My sister might come. I'm her ride home from school. She's going to PE class now. She hates having to dress for gym. I could go see if she wants to go.

LENNIE   Cool. Get going. We'll sort of casually drift toward the parking lot. We slip into my truck, then you girls can follow us in a few minutes. You know where my house is?

CECELIA   Yeah, Armando drove me by there one time. Your folks must make big bucks to afford a place like that.

LENNIE   Yeah, I guess. That's why they work so much. (*pause*) So that's why we shouldn't let the big old house get lonely, know what I mean?

CECELIA   I'll go grab my sister. Now don't you guys start the party without us. (*exits*)

LENNIE   So, what are we waiting for? Outta here! (*LENNIE, ARMANDO, and JAMES exit.*)

In LENNIE's living room, the five lounge around. They are playing music quite loudly, are drinking beer from the refrigerator, and hard liquor from his parents' liquor cabinet.

CECELIA   Lennie, this place is so cool. If I lived here, I don't think I'd ever want to leave.

ARMANDO (*to CECELIA*)   Hey, baby, you know what'd be even better? Why don't you go get some of that pot out of your car? We could really kick back!

JAMES   Sounds cool to me. You guys'll share, right? We'll make it up to you.

LENNIE   Yeah, for a party to be righteous, everybody needs to kick in a little something. I've got the place and the booze. Cecelia's got the pot. (*He turns to PATRICIA.*) What do you have, sweet thing?

ARMANDO   Oooooweeee! Come on, Patty, you know you've been checking him out.

PATRICIA (*laughing*)   Men are such pigs! But this drink sure tastes good. What's in it anyway?

LENNIE   Oh, I just mixed up some sweet liquor that I know most girls like. I did good, huh?

PATRICIA (*giggling*)   Oooh, yeah.

CECELIA   Well, I'm going out to the car. If I'm not back soon, send a posse, okay?

JAMES   You go, girl. (*CECELIA exits.*) Hey, crank up the music a little more. I can still hear.

LENNIE   Not too much, because we've got a lady next door who's always watching what goes on over here out her window. She griped once that she could feel her windows rattling when we had a party out by the pool. I don't really want her to know I'm in here. She knows when I get home from school.

ARMANDO   Is she good looking? Maybe James would like her? We could invite her over. Heck, my dad always says, "If you can't beat 'em, join 'em!" (*They all laugh.*)

The neighbor is watching out her window as CECELIA opens the door of her car. She checks her clock and nods to herself. She goes to the telephone.

DISPATCHER   Police Department. Can I help you?

NEIGHBOR   Uh, yes. I think there's a burglary in progress next door. There's a car out in front and someone just came out to it. But I know somebody's in the house because I hear music. Nobody's supposed to be home over there. The son is in school and the parents are at work until about seven.

DISPATCHER   Yes, ma'am. We'll send an officer right out there. What is the address of the house where the burglary is taking place?

NEIGHBOR   Uh, I think the number's 6110 Pine. Mine is 6108. I'll be watching for you. You better hurry, or they'll get away.

DISPATCHER   Yes, ma'am. And your name is?

NEIGHBOR   Mrs. Roderick Jones. Please hurry. We don't want this happening in this neighborhood.

DISPATCHER   No, ma'am. An officer is on the way.

CECELIA (*entering*)   Here's the stuff. Don't hog it now. We'll roll a couple of joints and share them, okay? We won't need too much with all the booze.

PATRICIA   Yeah, that stuff makes me forget the rules. I get dangerous.

LENNIE   Cool. But you're safe with us. We wouldn't do anything you wouldn't.

CECELIA rolls a couple of joints. LENNIE continues to pour drinks. They drink, chat, and share the joints. PATRICIA gets up and dances by herself, then says she feels like taking a nap.

PATRICIA   Lennie, where's your bedroom? Can I go in there and relax a little? I'm feeling a little dizzy.

LENNIE   Sure, Patty, it's right down the hall to the left. (*She starts down the hall.*) You want any company?

PATRICIA (*turning and looking at them all with a silly smile*)   Sure, that would be nice. You all wanna join us? (*LENNIE follows her down the hall.*)

ARMANDO   Well, she's feeling no pain. (*to CECELIA*) Is your sister always like that? Wow. I thought the stuff I heard around school was just trash.

CECELIA   Not always. She has to think the guy is cute first. But enough about her. You wanna dance with me? I get good when I get relaxed. (*They dance.*)

JAMES (*at the CD player fiddling with a stack of CDs*)   Well, I feel like just one shoe. I'm getting a headache. Maybe I'll go on home. (*Looks at his watch.*) Shoot, it's almost five o'clock. (*to ARMANDO and CECELIA*) Hey, you guys, sorry to be a wet blanket, but I gotta get home. I'll just walk, 'cause I gotta get the smell of liquor off my breath and this smoke out of my clothes. Tell Lennie thanks, and I'll see him tomorrow, okay?

ARMANDO   All right. Be cool. See ya. (*JAMES heads for the front door, opens it, and stops suddenly.*) Oh my God, there's a black and white out here. (*Turns toward CECELIA and ARMANDO.*) A cop's coming, you guys. What're we going to do now? Someone go get Lennie. It's his house. He can handle this.

CECELIA   I will. (*Heads down the hall.*) Hey, Lennie, Patty! A cop's here. Lennie, come on and talk to them!

LENNIE   Oh, no. Mrs. Jones must have called on us. That old biddy! (*Smooths out his clothes as he hurries toward the living room.*)

PATRICIA (*coming to the door of the bedroom*)   Oh, God. I don't want to get arrested. We weren't doing anything.

CECELIA   Yeah, your hair looks great like that, and pull down your shirt, will you? The cop probably won't care about that, but you smell like skid row!

PATRICIA   Well, you suck too. You dragged me over here. I'm only fifteen. You're supposed to look out for me. (*From the living room, the girls hear the OFFICER's voice calling toward them.*)

OFFICER   Girls, come on out. Now! (*They straggle in.*)

PATRICIA   You're not going to take us to jail, are you Officer? Honest, I didn't do anything. My sister dragged me here!

OFFICER   I'll ask the questions here. I've already called Lennie's parents at work. They're on their way right now. (*turning to JAMES*) And you, you say your name is James? And you're sixteen? Since I can't reach your mom, you'll have to come with me till we can reach her. I can't let you leave here under the influence like this. (*turning to ARMANDO*) And your dad is on his way over here to pick you up. (*turning to the girls*) I see you brought your own transportation. Who's the driver of the car?

CECELIA   I am, sir.

OFFICER   And may I see your driver's license?

CECELIA   I don't have it with me, sir. But it's at home. Honest. It's lying right on my dresser, isn't it Patty?

PATTY   You mean your learner's permit? Yeah, I think I saw it there.

OFFICER   I was afraid of that. Not only have you been drinking and are under the influence of substances, but you don't have a legal driver's license. For your safety, I'm going to take you into custody until we can meet with your parents, and the car will have to be towed to an impound yard.

CECELIA   Oh, gosh, no. My mom needs that car to get to work.

OFFICER   I'd say you've got a problem. And so do the rest of you.

Discussion

1. Why do you think Lennie would invite kids to his house when his folks are at work?
2. What is the motivation for the other kids to ditch and go to Lennie's house?
3. Why do you think Cecelia wants to provide the pot?
4. Why does Patricia blame her sister for getting her into this mess?
5. Is Mrs. Jones wrong in reporting them to the police?
6. How could the kids' parents get in trouble for what the kids did? Is that fair?
7. If these kids were bored and wanted to have a good time so badly, name other ways they could have entertained themselves without breaking laws.
8. Even though it might seem exciting and tempting, what is a good way to resist peer pressure to go along and not make enemies? What are some things you could you say to let them know you weren't avoiding them, but what they wanted to do?

Tell Them You're Staying At My House

CHARACTERS
PERRY, GUS, BRANDON, JEROME, MOM, DAD

MOM, DAD, and PERRY are watching television on Saturday evening. The phone rings.

PERRY   I'll get it. It's probably for me. (*into phone*) Oh, hey, just a minute, let me go into the kitchen so I can hear. (*He takes phone into kitchen.*) So, what's up?

GUS (*voice on phone*)   So, you coming, man? It's almost ten.

PERRY   Yeah, sure. But I gotta be careful. I think my folks are getting suspicious. Are we meeting in your garage, like last time?

GUS   Same as before. So are you coming?

PERRY   Okay. What I'm gonna do is take my sleeping bag and say I'm staying at your house tonight. Okay? I'll tell them we're gonna watch movies and shoot pool. They'll probably buy that. So if they call over there to check on me, can your sister answer the phone and pretend I'm there?

GUS   Yeah, but even better, we'll put the answering machine on. They'll think we're just screening the calls. Then you can call back. We'll check with the cell phone to see if there are any messages, and then you can call them from wherever. Cool, huh?

PERRY   That'll work. I'll get going now, and if something messes up, I'll call your cell phone, okay?

GUS   Okay, then. Hurry up.

PERRY, GUS, BRANDON, and JEROME have gathered in GUS's garage.

BRANDON   So, crew, we got work to do. The Twisters have tagged all down South Street. And it's ugly stuff. The people there are all upset. They're trying to blame it on us and they don't even know us for sure. So we gotta maintain our reputation for being the best.

JEROME   Yeah, but the cops are getting really busy there. We gotta get more clever than ever. Right? (*They all nod and mumble "uh-huh."*) WTLB has got to be all over, better, and where it can't be messed with. Are you all down with me on this?

ALL   We're down. For sure. (*They jam their clenched fists together in their special salute.*)

GUS   All right. Now, here's the plan. My folks think we're out here shooting some pool and listening to CDs, so that's what we'll do. They'll go to bed about eleven, and we'll still kick back for a while. Brandon, did you bring the forties?

BRANDON   Yeah, man. I got them. My friend who works at the little market handed them to me out the back door. I only got two, though.

GUS   Hey, that's okay. We don't want to get too messed up. We got work to do. We really should wait and drink them when we're done. Then we can celebrate for real.

PERRY   For sure, we got to wear gloves so we don't stain our hands. My mom saw that once and I had to tell her I was making a special project in shop class.

GUS   So, did you all bring paint? I got some spares at the swap meet. Heck, that guy'll sell to anyone. He just winks at me when I buy it.

BRANDON   Cool. I sorta five-fingered some from a garage sale. I've only got a couple of cans.

GUS (*taking out a cardboard box stored under the workbench full of spray paint cans*) Well, don't worry about it. This should last us a while.

JEROME That's good. We can do some really good work with that. Okay, let's kick back a while. When we decide to rest a little, I'll set this alarm clock. (*He holds it up.*) Does 2:30 seem about right? That'll give us about three hours of dark.

BRANDON Yeah. But I'd like to ease up now with a little outta the forty.

They play pool, listen to music, drink a little, then about midnight, sprawl on the couch, the floor, and an old overstuffed chair in the garage and doze off. The house gets quiet, for GUS's parents have gone to bed. Finally, at 2:30, the alarm goes off.

GUS Come on, up, up, you guys, it's time.

JEROME Huh, yeah, okay. Let me grab my stuff.

BRANDON So you guys agree, WTLB is going to be tagged all down First Street, and if we have time, we'll cover some of the stuff on South Street that the Twisters left. Bunch of speed freaks, they need us to fix up their "art."

PERRY But First Street is ours. I got a great plan for those overcrossings.

GUS So let's start at that first bridge, okay? Come on.

At the First Street Bridge, they carefully look up and down the street to make sure no cars are coming. They crouch in some bushes.

JEROME Okay, Perry, this one's yours. We'll keep a lookout.

GUS Go, Perry. Use the purple and black. We want everyone to know we were here.

BRANDON You got the gloves on?

PERRY Yeah, I'm cool. Watch, now.

PERRY steps over the bridge railing and hangs on while he sprays a W. He adds the T over a Twisters mark, and finishes the L and B. He signals he's done, the others creep out and admire his work, and they move on down the street. GUS decides they should split up so they can get more area covered, so two go on either side of the street. PERRY is near JEROME. They hear a car coming.

JEROME Perry, man, somebody's coming. Get outta sight!

PERRY Oh, no. (*They turn and dash into some tall weeds beside a building. A squad car slowly cruises by. It flashes its spot light on the new graffiti.*)

JEROME (*whispering*) Don't even move, man. (*The light passes above them, then goes to the other side of the street.*)

PERRY Oh, no. I hope Gus and Brandon heard them coming.

The patrol car stops, the officers get out, BRANDON and GUS run, but are caught, cuffed, and hauled away.

JEROME (*rising from weeds and brushing himself off*) Man, I hope they don't snitch on us. Let's get out of here!

PERRY Man, that was a close one. But we did some good work, huh?

Sunday evening at dinner, PERRY, MOM, and DAD sit at the dinner table.

MOM Perry, I thought you guys were just going to watch videos at Gus's. I tried to call, but I just got the answering machine. Don't they ever answer their phone?

PERRY Yeah, Mom, I got the message, but I didn't call back because I thought you guys would be asleep.

MOM Didn't you get any sleep at all? I'm glad you got up in time for dinner. (*She smiles at him and tousles his hair.*)

DAD Easy on him, honey. I mixed it up pretty good when I was his age.

MOM   But I get worried when he has such a hard time getting up for school. (*to DAD*) Oh, by the way, did you see all that ugly graffiti all over First Street? What kind of pigs would do that?

DAD   Yes, and I heard on the local news that the cops got two thugs in the act last night. The cops identified them as claiming to be some kind of a club. They called it a crew and said WTLB stood for Walk The Line Boyz. They can't even spell.

MOM (*turning to PERRY*)   Honey, do you know any of these delinquents who do this stuff?

PERRY (*looking down at his plate*)   Mom, why would I know anyone like that?

DAD   Well, Perry, I hope we can trust you. I'd be furious if my kid did anything like that. He'd never get my permission to get a driver's license, and you can bet I'd forget about the custom car I had in mind for him.

Discussion

1. Why has Perry risked his parents' trust to hang out with the tagging crew?
2. If Perry continues to hang out with his tagging crew, what is likely to happen to him?
3. If you were Perry's parents and you found out about his tagging, what would be your conflicts?
4. If you were one of the property owners whose buildings and fences got tagged, how would you feel?
5. If communities set aside a special tagging art area, do you think taggers would quit secretly marking up other property?
6. If you were a judge, what do you think would be corrective punishment for taggers?
7. If you were tempted to tag, what could you do instead that would be constructive instead of destructive?

We do what we want

Defy Authority

CHARACTERS
RICHARD, HOWARD, JACK, ANDREA, MOM, MISS LANDRY

RICHARD is getting ready for school.

MOM   Richard, you're not going to school wearing that t-shirt. It's embarrassing to me to have you be seen in it.

RICHARD   There you go. Nagging me again. I get so sick of that. You know Uncle Henry sent me this as a souvenir.

MOM   It's disgusting.

RICHARD   You're so out of it. Times change. Besides, I have rights. Just because it says "Shut up, bitch," doesn't mean I'm talking to anyone special. Lighten up.

MOM   Well, if you get in trouble at school, don't blame me. And wipe up that mess on the counter.

RICHARD   Yeah, yeah, yeah. (*Ignores mess. Slams door on his way out.*)

In first period, MISS LANDRY has passed out copies of Ray Bradbury's book Fahrenheit 451.

MISS LANDRY (*to class*)   Have any of you read this book before?

RICHARD   Yeah. It sucks.

MISS LANDRY   Why do you say that, Richard?

RICHARD   Because it's boring. It doesn't have any pictures, and who cares about a jerk that works in a fire station? Hey, if books are boring, they should be burned.

MISS LANDRY   I'm sorry you feel so negative toward reading, Richard. If you could get interested in what Ray Bradbury has to say in this book, I think you'd find that he raises some serious questions about who should control our thinking.

RICHARD   Well, you forcing this book on us is a way to control our thinking.

MISS LANDRY (*annoyed*)   Richard, I am teaching school-district and state-authorized curriculum here. This is a public school, and we teach ethics and ideas that support the American way of life. But we can't guarantee to please everyone all the time. So this will be the end of this conversation.

JACK   You tell him, Miss Landry.

RICHARD (*turning on JACK*)   Hey, *nobody* tells me what to do. I'm a free person. School is forced on me. (*He stands and removes his jacket in front of everyone, revealing his t-shirt.*)

ANDREA   Miss Landry, I object to that sexist shirt!

MISS LANDRY   And so do I. Young man, I'm going to have to ask you to go to the office. It's not okay for you to wear a shirt in here that is so blatantly offensive to women.

RICHARD   Hey, my uncle gave me this. You can't tell me what to wear!

MISS LANDRY   Well, young man, I have rights too, and so does Andrea. And we don't have to have you broadcast disrespect for women on your shirt. So pick up your stuff and head for the office!

RICHARD   This place sucks! (*He gathers his jacket and backpack and stalks out of the room.*)

HOWARD   Miss Landry, no offense intended, but doesn't he have the right to free expression?

MISS LANDRY   Yes, he does, but he also has to accept the consequences of his actions. The school board has established a dress code, which I'm sure you've heard of. It prohibits clothing that is racist, sexist, gang oriented, promotes drugs, and so forth.

ANDREA   And that covers filthy language, too, doesn't it?

RICHARD enters the class and stalks to his desk. He is wearing his shirt inside out.

MISS LANDRY   Yes, it does.

HOWARD   But what does it hurt anybody if kids are just talking and they use the "f" word and they're not calling anybody names or anything? Isn't that their business?

ANDREA   Yeah, the stuff is in the lyrics on CDs and everywhere.

RICHARD   Yeah, nobody has the right to tell me what I can say. Man, that's fascism.

JACK   Hey, dude, you forget that other people have rights, too. And I got rights not to have to listen to you mouth off.

HOWARD   Easy, man, we're just trying to have a discussion here.

ANDREA (*to Jack*)   Yeah, how does it hurt you what I say? Mind your own business unless I'm talking to you. You trying to be a preacher, or something?

JACK   Well, I noticed you were the first one to object to his t-shirt.

MISS LANDRY   Okay, class. We need to wind this down and get on with the book here. None of us wants other people getting in our business and telling us what to do. If we were the only ones living on earth, we could do anything, disgusting or not, anytime, and there'd be nobody to care. But there are lots of us, and we have to learn to work together.

RICHARD   But nobody has the right to tell us what to do. The cops stop you at night and want to know where you are going, the politicians all are crooks, stores try to rip you off, and they've got those nosy cameras everywhere. Man, this society is totalitarian. The only way to be free is to defy authority. Screw them.

JACK   So if I decide I don't like your looks, I can get in your face and tell you where to go?

HOWARD   Hey, that would be cool. Does that mean I could tell my dad his rules stink? Hey, if I want to use the car, everybody better get out of my way. (*He laughs.*)

MISS LANDRY   Okay, I hate to sound like a teacher here, but we all know we have to follow some rules. Where would we be if there were no traffic laws? People would be killed all over the place. But the trick is, where do one person's rights infringe on the rights of someone else? Like Richard's shirt. It set a disrespectful tone which infringed on the rights of women to be in a respectful environment. Do you agree?

HOWARD   Yeah, I see the point. I wouldn't want anyone being disrespectful to my mom or sister.

ANDREA   And the dirty words, they make me feel ashamed. Like the people saying them around me don't care if they offend me. If they don't care if they offend me, they must not think very highly of me. I bet they wouldn't talk that way around a priest or minister or judge.

MISS LANDRY   You're getting it. So now, back to the book. *Fahrenheit 451* talks about how much government should control what people read, think, and feel. And, Richard, it shows a time when someone actually *had* to defy authority. But when is the right time?

Discussion

1. Should Richard's mom have stopped him from wearing the offensive t-shirt to school? Why or why not?
2. Would it ever be okay to wear that t-shirt where others could see it?
3. In what way might using dirty words about sex be disrespectful to others? How about profane words that deal with religion? How about dirty words that deal with going to the bathroom?
4. Why might people deliberately and carelessly use dirty words around others?
5. When might using dirty words be punishable and against the law? Why would laws like this exist?
6. When should the authority of parents be respected? Are there ever times when parents might overstep their authority? When?
7. Are there ever times when young people should defy authority? What kinds of wrongs should not be tolerated? What are proper ways to deal with these wrongs?
8. How do you respect the rights of others?

What Have You Done to Yourself?

CHARACTERS
BETH, SHAWNA, EVAN, HUGH, NURSE

At lunch time, students lounge around outdoor tables.

BETH   So, Shawna, when are you gonna get your tongue pierced?

SHAWNA   Hmmph! Are you kidding? My mom won't let me do that.

BETH   Why not? It's your body. Mine didn't like it at first, but then she mellowed out. I convinced her that every generation does their thing. She couldn't argue with me, because I know she did some goofy stuff when she was a flower child.

SHAWNA   Really? Mine is not like that. And I think I'm glad, because I don't even have to think about it.

EVAN   Don't you even want any tattoos? I love it when girls want to show me their tattoos, especially the ones they've had done under their clothes.

BETH   You guys! You don't have to be so blunt about it.

HUGH   Why not? Why have a tattoo if nobody is going to look at it? Hey, it's body art. And the body is beautiful. What's there to be ashamed of?

SHAWNA   Yeah, I've heard that one before. I like to keep some things private.

BETH   What for? Hey, why be so up tight? Life is to live. Go for it. That's what my mom says anyway. So, I don't complain about her boyfriends, and she doesn't complain about what I do to my body.

EVAN (*to BETH*)   So where else you got piercings besides your tongue and lower lip? (*teasing*) Huh? Huh? I know of some girls who get their nipples pierced and other places I won't even mention here.

HUGH   And guys who have theirs done, too.

SHAWNA   Yeah, I've heard of all that. And tattoos on all those places too. Man, that's really far out. And the same kids will cringe if they've got to get a shot against hepatitis from the doctor. I don't get it.

BETH   I guess you don't understand unless you do it. Hey, it gives you some kind of control. You gotta do everything else to please people, but at least you can do what you want to your own body. Hey, I love the butterfly on my back. And I think it looks good when I wear halter tops. So do other people.

SHAWNA   I didn't mean to judge anyone. Everybody to their own taste. I just wonder how sanitary it all is.

EVAN   I had the one in my tongue taken out because it was always getting infected. The doctor said if I got a bad enough infection, I might have to have part of my tongue cut out. No way, man.

BETH   Oh, don't be a wuss. All you have to do is keep them clean. A little peroxide once in a while.

HUGH   But what about when people, you know, French kiss? Can't you get some kind of a disease from somebody else's mouth?

BETH   Hey, that's easy. Don't kiss anybody with scuzzies around the mouth.

EVAN   Well, people do other stuff with their mouths, too, if you know what I mean. What if they have some kind of a disease and it gets into your mouth? Can that happen?

HUGH   I heard about a girl who got herpes blisters clear down her throat from oral stuff she did with her boyfriend.

SHAWNA   You guys are grossing me out. Hey, if you haven't made holes in yourself, then you won't have so much to worry about.

HUGH   Yeah, yeah, yeah. And you can go sit on your chair and be afraid of everything, and life will pass you by. Hey, some of the fun comes with risks.

EVAN   Man, this conversation sounds like a bunch of old people. I think we should ask the nurse in health class. She should give us the straight truth.

BETH   Yeah, that's next period. Let's ask her. Evan, you ask her. Nobody will laugh at you.

In health class, the NURSE has begun a lecture on the dangerous behavior that can risk infection for HIV.

NURSE   So, students, let's review, and then you can ask questions. Remember, anytime blood, semen, vaginal fluid, or mother's milk of an infected person can get into the body openings of someone else, we have a chance of infection. Those body openings are the mouth, the genitals, the anus, and breaks in the skin. And if a person already is infected with other sexually transmitted infections, it makes it easier for HIV to get into another person because of sores or lesions from the other diseases.

EVAN   Uh, can I ask a question for my friends who are too embarrassed to ask?

BETH   You know you're the one who needs to know, Evan.

NURSE   Okay, okay. The truth is, you *all* need to know. So of course, Evan, ask any question you want.

EVAN   Does having piercings in your mouth put you in any more danger?

NURSE   It depends on what goes into your mouth. (*Everyone laughs nervously.*) If a piercing has left an opening of any kind for the four body fluids from another to get in, there could be transmission of infection.

BETH   Oh, my gosh. But can't you tell who's sick and who isn't? I mean, I don't kiss anybody anywhere who isn't clean.

NURSE   Well, that would be fine if you could always tell when someone was infected, but you can't tell by looking. Hepatitis and HIV spread easily by body fluids in body openings, and you can't tell if someone is infected without doing careful testing.

HUGH   We got your point, but that means tattoos are safe, right?

BETH   Please, say yes.

NURSE   Well, it depends. It depends on who does the tattoo, if they use sterilized needles, if they use only brand new ink out of the bottles, then don't dump any leftover ink back into the bottles. It *is* enough of a problem that blood banks often exclude the blood of people who have tattoos done. They screen them carefully.

EVAN   So if my friend does it real cheap, would that pass?

NURSE   It could pose a problem.

BETH   Why is it that everything that is so fun can be so dangerous?

SHAWNA   Maybe it depends on what your definition of "fun" is. I have lots of fun, and I don't have any tattoos or piercings.

BETH (*getting irritated*)   Well, some people choose to do things other ways. This is a free country!

NURSE   Yes, it's legal to get piercings and tattoos in some states if you get parental permission. But because it can be so dangerous, practitioners who do these things can get in trouble with the law if they perform these acts on minors.

HUGH   Another thing—it makes me mad when jobs get all up in your face about not allowing piercings and tattoos that show at work. What business is that of theirs?

EVAN   Can I answer that? My mom runs a secretarial service. Those business people want real clean-cut looking employees.

NURSE   Yes, they can do that. They can set their own dress codes, and that can include obvious tattoos and piercings.

HUGH   But isn't that unfair? You know, discrimination?

NURSE   It's only illegal for them to discriminate on the basis of race, religion, national origin, age, and gender and maybe a few other things that have to do with ability to do the job. These tattoos and piercings are a matter of personal choice, but with that choice comes other people's right to approve or disapprove. Do any of you know if a tattoo can be removed?

EVAN   Yeah, I know a girl who broke up with a guy and wanted his name off. It cost a bunch, and it hurt when they sizzled it off with a laser.

NURSE   Yes, think carefully before making such a permanent change to your body. Fads come and go. You might have as much fun expressing your individuality in some other non-permanent way.

BETH   Well, I still think piercings and tattoos are sexy. So I'll take the risk.

SHAWNA   That's your choice, but if there are complications, and you get hepatitis or HIV, it could lead to death. Death isn't very sexy.

HUGH   But it'll never happen to us, right?

NURSE   That's what a lot of people tell themselves, but those victims out there said that too.

Discussion

1. Why do you think the law in some states requires parental permission for young people to get tattoos or have themselves pierced?

2. Do you think tattoos and piercings are a fad of the current generation? Do you think they will ever go out of style?

3. Do you think young people would still want piercings or tattoos if no one else would ever see them?

4. What other ways could young people express their individuality without health risks or permanently marking their bodies?

What Set You With?

CHARACTERS
AUSTIN, CURTIS, GANG BANGER 1, GANG BANGER 2, MARY (AUSTIN's sister), DAD

AUSTIN is new in the neighborhood. CURTIS lives in the same apartment complex and belongs to the Upside Boyz gang. AUSTIN and DAD are fixing dinner in the kitchen of their apartment.

AUSTIN   So, how's the new job seem?

DAD   Okay, so far. A couple of the guys showed me around. But the problem is, this first week is the last time I get to work days. Next week, I've got to work swing shift. When you're low man on the totem pole, you gotta take the shifts nobody else wants. I hate having you and Mary by yourselves here at night. Especially in a new neighborhood.

AUSTIN   Well, I am sixteen. I ought to be old enough to handle things. But Mary gets on my nerves. Just because she's a year older, she thinks she can boss me around and do anything she wants.

DAD (*dishing up bowls of stew from a kettle on the stove*)   Here, set these on the table, will you?

AUSTIN (*carrying the bowls to the table*)   I thought girls were supposed to do this stuff.

DAD (*calling*)   Mary? Mary!

MARY (*Enters from the living room where she has been talking on the phone.*)   What, Dad? I was just on the phone with Grandma.

DAD   Pour some milk for you and your brother, will you?

AUSTIN   Yeah, you kept talking to Grandma because you knew we were in here getting dinner, didn't you?

MARY   Shut up, Austin. (*pouring the milk and carrying it to the table*) Come on, Dad. Let's eat. (*They sit down, to AUSTIN.*) By the way, you look dorky wearing that fake gold chain that Grandma gave you. Personally, I think you might get more attention than you want if you walk around in this neighborhood with that flashing. I see some scumbags around here hanging out. Even if you are a pain in the butt, I don't want you getting jumped.

AUSTIN (*fingering the chain around his neck*)   Dad, see that? She cares. But seriously, Mary, dear, dear sister, you may be older but I'm taller, and I can take care of myself.

DAD   Yeah, I've noticed some gang-types cruising around myself. If this job works out, we'll move as soon as we can. (*He pauses and looks at both of them.*) After your mom suffered for so long … (*His voice trails off.*)

MARY (*comforting him*)   It's okay, Dad. We know. We're old enough to have some sense.

DAD   Well, will you two please promise me that you'll stay inside at night? You know, do your homework, rent some movies, something. Just don't go out on the street, okay? You're all I've got left. (*They eat in silence.*) And please don't invite anyone in till we get better acquainted around here, okay?

The next afternoon, AUSTIN is walking home from the convenience market with a gallon of milk. A car pulls up along side him with GANG BANGER 1 and GANG BANGER 2 in it.

GANG BANGER 1   Hey! Hey, you! (*AUSTIN turns, sees them, then tries to ignore them and keep walking.*) Hey, you deaf? Hey!

AUSTIN (*stopping and facing them*)   You talking to me?

GANG BANGER 1   You're new around here?

AUSTIN   Well, sorta. What's up?

GANG BANGER 2 (*eyeing AUSTIN'S gold chain*)   What set you with?

AUSTIN   What? (*Begins to back away.*)

GANG BANGER 2   I *said*, What set you with? You hard of hearing, or what?

AUSTIN   Hey, I'm not with any set. I just mind my own business.

GANG BANGER 1 (*opening car door and stepping out*)   Well, then, I need your chain.

AUSTIN (*turning to leave*)   No. Hey, no.

GANG BANGER 2 (*Jumps out of car and grabs AUSTIN from behind, holding his arms down. AUSTIN drops the gallon of milk and GANG BANGER 2 kicks it to the side, to GANG BANGER 1.*)   Grab it, man. Yank it off him. (*GANG BANGER 1 breaks the chain trying to pull it off, and it leaves a scrape mark on AUSTIN'S neck.*) You got it?

GANG BANGER 1   Got it! (*Punches AUSTIN in the stomach.*) Thank you, punk. (*Both GANG BANGERS get back in the car and speed off.*)

At the apartment, MARY opens the door. CURTIS, whom she met in the laundry room, is carrying her basket of clean clothes.

MARY   Thank you very much.

CURTIS   Hey, gotta make the new neighbors feel welcome.

MARY   I'd invite you in, but my dad says no one's to be here but me and my brother. (*Looks intently at CURTIS.*) Say, what's that tattoo on your hand? That looks like a gang insignia. You belong to a gang?

CURTIS   When you live in this neighborhood, that's how you survive. A few of us just look out for each other. That's all. (*AUSTIN approaches.*) So who's this?

AUSTIN (*gesturing toward CURTIS*)   Mary, who's this? You know what Dad said. (*Rubs his scraped neck.*)

MARY (*Looks intently at him.*)   What's wrong, Austin? Hey, your chain is missing! I told you not to flash it around here. What happened?

AUSTIN (*Glances toward CURTIS.*)   Some punks jacked me. Asked me what set I was with.

CURTIS   Yep, that sounds like the punks that live over on the other side of the freeway. They're the Crushers. You're lucky that's all they did. I take it this is your brother, Mary?

MARY   Oh, sorry. Yeah, Austin, meet Curtis. He lives here in the complex. He just helped me carry this laundry home.

AUSTIN   Okay. Thanks for helping my sister. You know those guys that did this?

CURTIS (*nods*)   Hey, that's why, here in the complex, we take care of business ourselves.

AUSTIN   You mean, you belong to a gang, too? (*turning to MARY*) I don't like the way this is going. We better get inside.

CURTIS   Wait up. Wait up. If your sister wasn't so fine, I'd let you sink on your own, but she doesn't need any grief. I got a way you can take care of your business around here. The Upside Boyz may want to check you out.

MARY (*to AUSTIN*)   Oh, no. I don't think so. Dad would flip. (*turning to CURTIS*) Well, we gotta go in. Thanks for helping me. See you. Come on, Austin. (*MARY and AUSTIN exit.*)

CURTIS turns away, then is approached in the quad area of the complex by several other members of the Upside Boyz. They discuss AUSTIN and agree that they should offer him membership. The next day after school, they approach Austin in the complex's entrance.

CURTIS   Hey, Austin, hold up. We want to talk to you. (*Several Upside Boyz gather around AUSTIN.*)

AUSTIN   What's up?

CURTIS   We decided to see if you'd cut it with us.

AUSTIN   What do you mean?

CURTIS   We can offer you protection. And your sister is going to need it, too. The Crushers are into some heavy stuff.

AUSTIN   Oh, God.

CURTIS   So you wanna hear about it?

AUSTIN   I guess so.

CURTIS   Okay, here's the deal. You do us a favor, you know, to show you're for real. If you pass our little test, we initiate you. Then you're in and your life picks up some speed. The Crushers won't likely mess with you if they know they gotta deal with all of us.

AUSTIN   What kind of favor do I have to do?

CURTIS   First, you gotta tag up their neighborhood, to show we're in charge. Then, you gotta make some money for us. We'll know stuff about you, and you'll know stuff about us, and we'll be like brothers. And then we'll know we can trust you.

AUSTIN   I don't think I can do all that.

CURTIS   You want your chain back? You want your sister safe? You can do what you got to do, man! We all do.

Discussion

1. What are Austin's conflicts?
2. Is there any way Austin can live in the new neighborhood in peace without joining a gang? Explain.
3. If Austin did join the Upside Boyz, what bad things might happen to him?
4. Is there any way Mary can be safe in the apartment complex controlled by Curtis and the Upside Boyz? Explain.
5. Should Austin report the theft of the necklace and the assault from the gang bangers to the police? Why or why not?
6. If you were Austin and Mary's father, what would you do about your children being approached by gang members?
7. Can managers of apartment complexes legally throw out gang members?
8. If you lived in this neighborhood, how would you handle this situation?

Being picked on

Bullying — What Can You Do About It?

CHARACTERS
DEIDRE, DIANNE, CAROLINE, MOM, VICE PRINCIPAL ADAMS

DEIDRE, a short, slender sophomore, is a quiet student and a teacher's aide in homemaking class. She grades quiz papers and passes out materials for the teacher. DIANNE and CAROLINE think she's stuck up. DEIDRE is walking alone to the bus stop after school. DIANNE and CAROLINE begin to follow her.

CAROLINE (*loud enough for DEIDRE to hear*)   Hey, Dianne, isn't that that uppity girl from homemaking?

DIANNE   Yeah, I think so. She thinks she's something special just because she's the teacher's aide.

CAROLINE   For sure. She needs to get real. You know what I mean?

DIANNE   Like what? (*DEIDRE hears them and begins to walk a little faster.*)

CAROLINE   Hey, look! She's on the run. She's trying to avoid us.

DIANNE (*calling*)   Hey, girl. Girl! Hey, you up there, from homemaking. Wait up. We just want to talk to you. (*DEIDRE hurries even faster.*)

CAROLINE   This is making me mad. She's ignoring us. Look, she's getting up to the bus stop. (*turning to look for the bus, then checking her watch*) Too bad. It won't be here for ten more minutes. Are you up to teaching her a lesson?

DIANNE   Like what?

CAROLINE   You know, to show us some respect. (*calling to DEIDRE*) Hey, wait, girl. We just want to talk to you a minute. (*DEIDRE has reached the bus stop and turns to face them wondering what to do.*)

DIANNE (*getting close*)   Hey, what's your name, anyway? You're in homemaking, aren't you?

DEIDRE (*shyly*)   Yes, I am. Fifth period. You two are in there too, aren't you?

CAROLINE (*taking a stance in front of DEIDRE*)   You're darned right we are. And you're the teacher's pet, aren't you?

DEIDRE   No! All I do is help out the teacher for some skill credits. I'm no pet. I just do what the teacher tells me.

DIANNE   You grade quizzes, don't you?

DEIDRE   Well, yeah, that's part of my job. And I sort supplies, and run errands, and pass out stuff. (*Tries to lighten up the situation.*) You know, a regular old gopher.

CAROLINE   Funny. Real funny. But anyway, that gives me an idea. We got a job we need you to do for us.

DEIDRE (*Looking nervously down the street, she sees the bus coming a few blocks away.*)   Oh, yeah? What's that?

DIANNE   You could help us out in that class.

DEIDRE (*relaxing a little*)   Yeah? How's that?

CAROLINE   Well, when we take those quizzes, you could see that we get high grades.

DEIDRE   What do you mean? I just grade them. I don't have any control over the questions.

CAROLINE No, dummy. We mean, you know, kinda fix our answers for us. You know, give us high grades. The teacher will just mark whatever you write in the gradebook. You can do that for us now, can't you?

DEIDRE You want me to cheat for you? I can't do that! Then I'd get in trouble. The teacher trusts me.

DIANNE That's the point. You could get away with it. But I don't feel like talking about this all day. You'll do it or you'll wish you had. We don't ask favors very often, but when we do, we expect people to respect us! So here comes your bus! You understand what you're going to do for us?

CAROLINE Yeah, don't forget, life can be good for you, or very, very bad. Get it? (*turning to DIANNE*) So, we're gonna get top grades for a change tomorrow on the quiz, right? (*They give each other high fives.*)

DIANNE We will or else. Won't we, miss teacher's aide? See you tomorrow! (*DEIDRE turns away from them and quickly gets on the bus.*)

The next day, DEIDRE tells her mother she feels sick and wants to stay home from school. Her mother accepts her story because she's never lied before. Then she feels ashamed, so after her mother has gone to work, she takes the bus and gets to school late but is there for homemaking class. Sure enough, CAROLINE and DIANNE are there, and when DEIDRE is asked to pass out the quiz papers, they both look warningly at DEIDRE. DEIDRE grades the quizzes honestly, and the next day, both girls get their papers back with what they have earned, Ds. After class, they corner DEIDRE in the hall. Another student in the class stops a short distance away and sees what is going on.

CAROLINE Well, you suck-up, looks like you've got something coming!

DEIDRE (*trying to push past them*) Leave me alone, you guys. I just do what I'm told.

DIANNE Well, you didn't do what we told you to do! That was stupid! (*pushing her up against the wall*) Smack her, Caroline! Hurry up before someone comes.

CAROLINE (*giving DEIDRE a couple of punches to the stomach, then grabbing her by the hair and throwing her to the floor*) There, you teacher's pet! How's it feel? Huh? Next time it'll be even worse. (*The other student hurries into a nearby classroom. Vice Principal Adams rounds the corner and sees Deidre struggling to get up, but only glimpses Caroline and Dianne ducking around the corner. He doesn't quite recognize them.*)

ADAMS Here, let me help you up. Come on with me to the office. Who did this to you? (*DEIDRE is silent as they walk to the office.*) Come on. You need to tell me. We can't have this kind of behavior in our school.

DEIDRE (*sitting down in the office*) No. It was nothing. Just let it go. But let me catch my breath, will you?

ADAMS Let me look at your schedule and see what class you just came out of. (*Finds her schedule on the computer.*) Oh, here it is. Homemaking. Was it someone in homemaking?

DEIDRE I'm sorry, I can't say. I'm not sure of their names, and if I tell, they'll get in trouble and really cause me problems later. Let's just drop it, okay?

ADAMS I think I know who it might be. There were two of them, weren't there? (*DEIDRE just looks at the floor.*) Well, I need to call a parent. You live with your mom? (*DEIDRE nods.*) Okay, what's the number?

Later that evening, MOM tries to talk with DEIDRE.

MOM Honey, you've got to give the names of the girls who did this! They'll just keep it up if they get away with it.

DEIDRE Mom, I can't. They want me to cheat for them on their quizzes in homemaking. I can't do that either. This whole thing makes me sick. Maybe I should just go live with

Dad. I can't beat two of them up. I'm not a fighter. Shoot, they've got other friends around school. Nobody seems to be able to do anything about them.

MOM   Well, maybe everybody does what you want to do. Nothing. Because you're afraid of what else they might do. But you've got a right to go to that school in peace. They're the ones that should be worried, not you.

DEIDRE   Yeah, it sounds good on paper, but that's not how it works in that school. Honestly, I don't know what to do, Mom, but I sure don't want to go back there with this mess.

Discussion

1.   What are Deidre's conflicts?
2.   Describe as many ways you can think of, both bad and good, that Deidre can handle this problem.
3.   Why would Caroline and Dianne be willing to hurt someone they don't even really know?
4.   Have Caroline and Dianne committed a crime? Do you think they have done this to other students?
5.   If Deidre gives their names, what can be done to stop Caroline and Dianne from ganging up on her again?
6.   Should the other student who witnessed the attack tell what she saw? Why or why not?
7.   How can Deidre's mom help her?
8.   What could the school do to put a stop to this violence, yet still do something to help Caroline and Dianne learn proper behavior?
9.   How would you handle the situation if you were the vice principal?

You Didn't See Nothin'

CHARACTERS
ARNIE, GEORGE, STEWART, CLERK

*ARNIE is on his way home from basketball practice when he sees GEORGE and
STEWART inside a convenience store. GEORGE is pointing a gun at the clerk and
STEWART is waving a piece of iron pipe.*

GEORGE   Don't screw us around, man. Just give us the cash. Give it!

CLERK   Don't shoot! Don't shoot! (*Opens the register.*)

STEWART (*Hops over counter and grabs wads of bills, then stuffs them into his jacket
pockets.*)   Git down on the floor, old man. Git down! And don't even think of calling
anybody for five minutes, you hear!

CLERK   Okay, man! (*Lies down on the floor behind the counter.*) Okay. Just take the
money. No sweat, man!

STEWART   Well, just to make sure! (*Raises the pipe and strikes the CLERK in the head.*)

CLERK   Ooof! (*Starts to struggle to his feet.*)

GEORGE   Come on, man! Move your butt! (*They hurry out the door and see ARNIE
outside on the sidewalk staring at them.*)

STEWART   What's this? George, there's a witness! What'll we do?

GEORGE (*stopping a moment to stare back at ARNIE*)   What're you looking at? We were
just in there trying to buy cigarettes but the guy wanted to card us.

STEWART   So mind your own business! You didn't see nothin'! Did you? (*Raises the pipe
over his head and takes a few steps toward ARNIE.*)

ARNIE (*backing up and raising his hands in defense*)   Hey, I'm cool, man. I was looking
the other way. I didn't see anything.

GEORGE (*nervously*)   Come on, Stewart, we gotta split. A car is coming, man. Come on!

GEORGE and STEWART hurry out of sight down the alley.

ARNIE (*Steps to store doorway and sees the CLERK leaning against the counter and
rubbing the back of his head.*)   Are you all right, man? Did that guy hit you?

CLERK   Yeah! The tall, skinny one smacked me on the back of the head. I gotta call the
cops.

ARNIE   Where's your phone? I can call 911 for you.

CLERK (*handing him the phone from under the counter*)   Yes, please. Did you see them?

ARNIE (*lying*)   No, not really. (*Speaks into phone.*) There's been a robbery. And a guy got
hit on the head with a pipe. Come quick. (*pause while he listens to dispatcher*) You
know. The little market across from the park. Freddie's Place, I think it's called. (*pause*)
Oh, please, I'd rather not give my name. Are you on the way? Good! (*Hangs up the
phone and addresses the CLERK.*) They're on the way. I gotta go now. (*Starts for the
door.*)

CLERK   Hey, please, wait a minute. You could tell them what you saw. Please?

ARNIE   Sorry, man. Those guys are really bad news. They're famous for terrorizing
everybody. I don't want to get hurt too! Sorry, man. I didn't see anything.

Discussion

1. What is Arnie's conflict?
2. What are all the ways you can think of, both bad and good, that he can deal with this conflict?
3. What will happen if he does nothing?
4. What may happen if he tells the cops who he saw robbing the store?
5. What is the right thing for him to do?
6. Why do you think George and Stewart act the way they do?
7. Why have George and Stewart been able to develop a reputation for terrorizing people?
8. How does this hurt all of the people in the neighborhood?
9. What might convince George and Stewart to quit robbing and terrorizing people?
10. If you saw a crime in progress, what would you do?

"Those People" Gotta Go

CHARACTERS
CLARK, TINA, EDDIE, TRAN, SUE, MRS. EMERSON

Veterans' Day approaches and MRS. EMERSON is discussing the Vietnam War. TRAN has been in the United States for three years, while SUE was born in Los Angeles. CLARK and his dad belong to a white supremacist organization.

MRS. EMERSON   So, can any of you tell me why the United States sent military personnel to Vietnam in the first place?

TINA   Well, my dad, he's a veteran, says it was for freedom.

MRS. EMERSON   Whose freedom do you think that was?

EDDIE   Who knows, but a whole bunch of guys died over there and became dopers, like my uncle. Man, he's really messed up.

MRS. EMERSON   Yes, most people agree that the war was a tragic period in American history, but it's important that we understand why the United States sent soldiers over there in the first place. Can anybody tell me, then, why we fought Hitler in World War II?

CLARK   Hey, Hitler wasn't so bad. He was just trying to cleanse the earth of, you know, unsavory people. Think how much better off we'd be today if he'd been able to finish.

TINA   That's sick. Don't you know anything?

CLARK   I know that it's about survival of the fittest, and saving the American way. We got so many foreigners here, we're not even Americans anymore. I know *that*, Miss Smarty Pants.

MRS. EMERSON   Hold it. We're not going to call names or be disrespectful to anyone here. If we trace back far enough, we're all immigrants here. Native Americans have been here the longest, of course, but we need to get back to the subject. Why did we send troops to Vietnam?

SUE   My family's from Vietnam. My family came to escape communism. They wanted to take away our rights to run our own country and tell us we couldn't go to church.

MRS. EMERSON   That's right. We were trying to help another country maintain a democracy.

CLARK   Well, they shoulda stayed there. They shoulda fought their own battles. They killed Americans.

EDDIE   Yeah, my mom says it was an immoral war. But I never understood what she meant. How could a war be immoral? I thought that just had to do with sex. (*Several laugh.*)

MRS. EMERSON   I can see that we have a lot of learning to do to understand the facts of America's historical involvement in wars that were primarily to help other countries. Think about this, will you? Very simply, communism sounds good on the surface, because it suggests that everyone will share and no one will need. But people tend to corrupt idealistic beliefs like that. How it really worked out was that a few got to decide what was good for everyone else. I think if I told you how you had to think and what you had to believe, you'd say I was violating your rights.

TINA   My dad says that we couldn't even be talking like this if it weren't for soldiers willing to put their lives on the line.

CLARK   But do all the foreigners have to come here? I say, America for Americans!

TINA   You know, you're really a doofus, aren't you? Your family came here once and were the foreigners.

SUE   I was born here just like you. You're ignorant.

MRS. EMERSON   That's enough of that. I'm going to show you a film now about the Vietnam Wall in Arlington National Cemetery. Over 50,000 names are on that wall, and they were not much older than you when they went to serve their country because they were asked to help stop the spread of communism. Communism's goal was to take over the world. The South Vietnamese asked us to help them fight back, so we did. But the important part about Veterans' Day, is that we honor the men and women who were willing to serve their country. Please take notes in your journals about the film.

The film begins, and the students write in their journals. Later, MRS. EMERSON reads what CLARK has written.

CLARK's voice   "All those guys died to help a bunch of foreigners. And they married some of them, and now we've got mongrel kids in this country. And they just take over places. And the government gives them free money to start businesses. It's not fair."

After school, CLARK and EDDIE are walking home.

EDDIE   So, do you belong to some kind of a group? You've got slogans written all over your cammie jacket and backpack. Are you a skinhead or something?

CLARK (*looking intently at EDDIE*)   Hey, somebody's gotta resist the pollution of our country. But no, not really a skinhead. We can't be that obvious.

EDDIE   So what does your group do?

CLARK   I really can't say. We just try to preserve the American way.

EDDIE   Really? Not to be disrespectful, but what do you mean?

CLARK   You know, not mixing the races, law and order, no freeloaders, stuff like that.

EDDIE   That doesn't really sound too bad. Where do you guys get the bad reputation?

CLARK   People don't want to understand us. If you want to know more, I'll invite you to one of the meetings. You'll be sworn to keep your mouth shut about what we say, though.

EDDIE   Sounds cool. That Tran guy in class, you know, that can't speak English very well. He gets on my nerves. I hate it that he gets straight As. What do you do about someone like that? But Sue, she's smart and funny, and speaks perfect English.

CLARK   You let them know they're not welcome. I'll show you after class tomorrow. Okay?

After class the next day, TRAN leaves class with his backpack and begins to walk home alone. CLARK and EDDIE begin to follow him.

CLARK   Okay, Eddie, take notes. (*calling to TRAN*) Hey, if we took up a collection for plane tickets, would you go back to where you came from? (*TRAN hunches down and walks a little faster.*) Hey, slant eyes! Go home. (*TRAN ignores them.*)

EDDIE   Hey, man, it's not working.

CLARK   Okay, watch this. (*Runs up behind TRAN, yanks his backpack off, then kicks it into the street.*)

TRAN   No. Why you do that? (*Steps into the street to retrieve his backpack. When he tries to step back onto the sidewalk, CLARK shoves him hard to the pavement.*) Why you do that? I don't bother you.

CLARK   Because I want to, that's why. You don't belong here!

TRAN (*getting up*)   Why you do that? That's not fair. (*Assumes a fighting stance.*) You want to fight? Okay!

CLARK Oh, lookee, he wants to fight. (*Swings and socks TRAN in the jaw, but TRAN recovers and kicks him hard in the knee. CLARK hops around clutching his knee, to EDDIE.*) Man, get him! The little creep kicked me. Get him!

EDDIE But you hit him first.

CLARK Right on. He had it coming. Now are you a true American or not? Help me out, man.

Discussion

1. What is the basis for Clark's prejudice against "foreigners"?
2. What does the word "prejudice" really mean? How can you dislike someone if you don't even know them?
3. What does it mean to be an American?
4. How do you think Tran feels about how Clark talks in class?
5. What is the best way Eddie can handle this situation?
6. What would you do?

Nobody'll Mess with Me Now

CHARACTERS
MISTI, LOREN, NATHAN, EVAN, RUDY, BOBBI

LOREN stays after school for softball practice until five o'clock almost every day. He must walk home by himself, but today he is walking with his girlfriend, MISTI.

MISTI   You played real good today. I can tell you've been practicing your pitching. Did Coach say anything to you about it?

LOREN   Not really, but he gave me a thumbs up. I can't believe you stuck around all this time just to watch practice. That must be boring.

MISTI   Oh, it gives me a chance to get my homework done. I got my reading all done for English class when I wasn't admiring you.

LOREN   Ah, gee. Now I'm going to get stuck up. But you don't have to wait around.

MISTI   I know, but you need company on the way home, and besides, I'm a pretty good bodyguard.

LOREN   Hey, any guy would be glad to have you guard his body. (*They laugh, then stop when they see they have to walk by NATHAN and EVAN who are leaning against a vacant storefront.*) Uh-oh. I don't like the looks of this.

MISTI   Me neither. They say awful things about girls.

LOREN (*bristling*)   Did they say anything to you? The punks. If they did, I swear I'll … (*NATHAN and EVAN have spotted LOREN and MISTI so the two boys start toward them.*) It looks like they're coming our way.

MISTI   Let's just act like everything's fine. There are two of us. It is a public place.

LOREN   They better not say anything about you. (*He and MISTI continue walking toward the two boys.*)

NATHAN (*loudly*)   Evan! You see what I see? Uh-huh! Yum!

EVAN   Yeah, I do, but she's with that so-called athlete boyfriend of hers.

NATHAN   So maybe she likes him for his money. Shall we see? (*The four are face to face.*)

LOREN (*holding MISTI's hand and trying to step around them*)   Excuse us, please.

NATHAN   I'll take this. (*Grabs MISTI's wrist and pulls her away from LOREN, to EVAN.*) Jack him, Evan.

MISTI (*struggling to get away*)   Get your hands off me! Loren, help me!

LOREN (*lunging toward MISTI*)   Let her go! Let her go! Take my stuff! Just let her go!

EVAN (*yanking LOREN's backpack off and knocking him down*)   Hey, thanks. Don't mind if I do. (*Begins to search the backpack.*)

MISTI   Get your hands off me, you cretin! (*Twists so that his arm is across her face, then bites hard into the flesh of his inner arm.*)

NATHAN (*Writhes away, then turns and shoves her to the ground.*)   How dare you! (*Looks at his arm and sees blood oozing from the bite mark. Turns and kicks at her but she rolls away.*) She bit me. I'm bleeding! Evan, hurry up! Get his stuff! Man, I'm in pain.

EVAN   The jerk only has a twenty. (*Flings the backpack to the ground.*)

LOREN (*Rushes in a rage toward NATHAN.*)   I'll kill you, man. You're gonna get it! (*Swings, but NATHAN ducks.*)

NATHAN (*to EVAN*)   Come on, let's get out of here. The guy's nuts. They're both nuts.

EVAN (*as they head away, pointing at LOREN*)   Somebody's gonna die, and it ain't gonna be us, punk! You better watch your back! We got friends.

NATHAN   Come on, man. He doesn't deserve a warning. And I'm not done with that female of his yet, either. (*They exit.*)

MISTI (*getting up*)   Are you okay, Loren? I bit him a good one!

LOREN (*shaking his head*)   Yeah. I'm okay. How about you? (*Looks in his backpack.*) They got the twenty dollars I had. That's okay, but not what they did to you. Now they pushed me too far!

MISTI   Did you hear them threaten us? I don't like the sound of that. I've heard about the stuff they do. They're nobody to mess around with.

LOREN   I'm not going to take any crap off of them! This is war. (*They exit.*)

At home that night while his folks are out, LOREN finds his father's loaded revolver and slips it into his backpack. The next day in school, as he's stuffing his sweatshirt away, RUDY, who sits beside him in class, gets a glimpse of the gun. Later, at lunch, he tells his girlfriend BOBBI what he has seen.

BOBBI   You saw what?

RUDY   Shhh! Somebody'll hear you. It looked like a big old .45 to me.

BOBBI   Oh, no. This sounds like bad trouble. You heard about what happened yesterday, didn't you?

RUDY   You mean about how Loren got jacked on his way home?

BOBBI   Yeah, but it was even worse. That one guy grabbed Misti and jerked her around. She bit him. She told me this morning that those two guys threatened that somebody was gonna die. And Loren said, "This is war."

RUDY   So? It's none of our business. People who stick their noses into messes like this get hurt.

BOBBI   But if you told the principal, maybe he could head off the whole thing.

RUDY   Hey, if I get involved, they'll come after me. No way, baby. I plan to survive.

BOBBI   But you have to tell, Rudy. Lives are at stake here.

Discussion

1. Why doesn't Rudy want to tell that he saw a gun in Loren's backpack?
2. What is the best choice Rudy can make for the safety of everyone?
3. How has Loren made the problem worse by bringing a gun to school?
4. What could Misti do to help stop Nathan and Evan from terrorizing others?
5. Should Bobbi get involved as a third person who just heard about the gun? Why or why not?
6. What could school authorities or the police do about Nathan and Evan's criminal behavior?
7. What would you do if you knew about the gun?

Spreading Rumors

CHARACTERS

SHERYL, DAWN, MARYANN, PRINCIPAL, MR. JENKINS, MRS. JENKINS

MR. JENKINS has told SHERYL, DAWN, and MARYANN to stay after school to make up for disrupting class.

MR. JENKINS (*behind his desk, peering over his glasses*)   Girls, you must be quiet now and study your textbook reading for half an hour.

SHERYL (*snotty*)   But Mr. Jenkins, this isn't fair. You know we weren't the ones who threw the gym shoe around the room. It was those scuzzy boys.

DAWN   Yeah! How come you never blame them? You just pick on us because we're girls. My mom said teachers aren't fair to girls.

MARYANN   Will you guys shut up so we can get out of here! He won't start counting the half hour until we are quiet. Just shut up.

SHERYL   Well, you're the one talking, so *you* shut up!

MR. JENKINS   Please, girls. When you're ready to settle down, I'll start the timer. I can wait as long as necessary.

DAWN   Yeah, you'd like that, wouldn't you?

MARYANN   Dawn, for heaven's sake! (*The girls finally quiet down and are studying.*)

DAWN (*Deliberately drops her book on the floor, then leans over to pick it up.*)   Whoops. How clumsy! (*Notices MR. JENKINS looking at her.*) What are you looking at? My mom bought me this shirt, so don't stare.

MR. JENKINS   Ladies, you have twenty-one minutes more to go. (*Grades papers, looks at the clock, then gets up and erases the board.*)

DAWN (*whispering loudly to Maryann*)   Look at that. I can tell he wears jockey shorts. (*MR. JENKINS ignores her.*)

MARYANN   Shut up, will you? You're disgusting. Show a little respect. (*The girls study in silence a few more minutes and MR. JENKINS returns to his desk and grades papers.*)

Later, the three girls have stopped for sodas at the local fast food restaurant and are seated at a table outside.

SHERYL   Well, as sucky as it was, I got some of my reading done. Mr. Jenkins assigns way too much work. My dad says teachers shouldn't expect so much of kids. I mean, we do have lives.

DAWN   Unlike some geeky teachers. We were probably the thrill of his day.

MARYANN   But we did toss that shoe around.

SHERYL   Oh, lighten up, Maryann. That class is so boring. I mean, who cares about that ancient history stuff? He never cuts us any slack.

DAWN   And we gotta stay in there until June. How many more days is that?

SHERYL   Hey, I got an idea. I mean, it's pretty wild, but it might work. You know, he was in there with three healthy, decent looking girls, after school. Alone. Hint, hint. You get my drift?

MARYANN   What are you saying, Sheryl?

DAWN   Did he, sorta, you know, brush by your shoulders when he went up to the board? I think I saw him. And he did stare down my blouse.

MARYANN   Hey, nobody has to *stare* down your blouse. I'm surprised you haven't gotten pneumonia. Guys in class can barely get their eyes off you.

DAWN   Men are pigs. I can wear this if I want.

SHERYL   But back to my idea. What if he had to take a few days off? You know, to be investigated for unwanted touching of students.

MARYANN   But he hasn't done that. You'd be making up a big old lie. I don't like him much, but that would be just plain cruel.

SHERYL   Hey, if it's not true, nothing will really happen to him. We'll just get a few days' vacation. Substitutes are a lot more fun. And it would really break the monotony. What do you think?

DAWN   I'm down for it, but how would we do this? March into the principal's office and flat-out say Mr. Jenkins has been grabbing on us? They'll never believe that.

SHERYL   No, that wouldn't work. We've got to be delicate about this.

MARYANN   (*looking at her watch*)   You guys, I've got to get home. You don't need me to carry out your little scheme. I've gotta finish my homework. (*Rises, exits.*)

DAWN   She's such a chicken. Man. (*Reaches into her jacket for a tissue. Pulls out a carefully folded note from her boyfriend.*) Oh, that's where I put this. I was afraid I dropped it on the floor in some class. I wouldn't want anyone reading this.

SHERYL   Hey, that's it! We can write fake notes with fake names on them and pretend we're talking to each other about how Mr. Jenkins grabs on us.

DAWN   That's not much. It's got to say more than "grabs." Hey, how about we pretend some girl has been over to his house for help after school and they have sex. The note can talk about how she's pregnant.

SHERYL   Oh! That's wild. Let's do it. And tomorrow, we can sorta drop it secretly on the principal's secretary's desk.

SHERYL and DAWN carry out their plan the next day. MR. JENKINS is summoned to the principal's office right in the middle of class.

PRINCIPAL   Mr. Jenkins, something serious has come to my attention.

MR. JENKINS   Uh-oh. My family's okay, I hope.

PRINCIPAL   No, it's not about your family. But I'm going to have to send you home pending an investigation of your alleged improper conduct with a student.

MR. JENKINS   (*incredulously*)   What? What on earth are you talking about?

PRINCIPAL   Well, sir, when we have the hearing, you'll be able to review the evidence. Right now, though, I'd suggest that you seek counsel. The allegations are quite serious.

MR. JENKINS   (*shaking his head*)   I can't believe this! I haven't done anything but work hard trying to provide quality classes to my students. You could at least tell me what set off this whole situation.

PRINCIPAL   Mr. Jenkins, I hope the investigation will clear you, but we have written evidence that you have had sexual conduct with a student at your home.

MR. JENKINS   No way! No way! (*Rises and paces back and forth.*)

PRINCIPAL   I'm sorry, Mr. Jenkins. I have no other choice. When information like this comes to our attention, I must act on the side of safety for the students' sake.

Later, at home, MR. JENKINS speaks with his wife.

MR. JENKINS   I can't believe this. I have no idea where these charges could have come from.

MRS. JENKINS   Oh, honey, I'm so sorry. Even when your name is cleared, it'll never really be cleared, you know. But the attorney with the teachers' association may be able to shed a little light on what we can do when we see him tomorrow.

MR. JENKINS   Maybe we should just pick up and move out of this town. Even though I'm innocent, people will always wonder about me. My blood pressure can't stand this.

MRS. JENKINS   It's just so unfair. But you know what you always say: When good people don't fight back against evil, evil prevails. And this is really evil.

MR. JENKINS   I know you're right, but right now, I just feel really beaten down.

Discussion

1. Do you think Sheryl and Dawn realize the seriousness of what they've done to Mr. Jenkins? Why is what they've done so serious?
2. What should Maryann do when she finds out Mr. Jenkins is gone?
3. How do you think Mr. Jenkins feels? How do you think his wife feels?
4. What effect is the investigation of Mr. Jenkins likely to have on the quality of education for the students in his classes?
5. How would you feel if someone falsely accused you of a serious offense? What would be the proper way to deal with it?
6. How should Sheryl and Dawn be punished for what they have done?

He Got What He Deserved

CHARACTERS

RICK, HARRY, PETER, DELORES, SECURITY GUARD

RICK is standing in line for lunch behind DELORES.

RICK   Hey, Delores, can you see what they're having in there? I can't stand that spaghetti glue-like stuff!

DELORES (*turning and smiling*)   No, but the menu for the week said that today it was going to be pizza. You like that, don't you?

RICK   Well, yeah, but it's greasy. I'd like some salad.

DELORES (*Grabs RICK's arm and turns him around.*)   Hey, don't look back. Those creeps Harry and Peter are there. (*RICK starts to turn to look, but DELORES yanks him back around. HARRY and PETER, with their hands on their hips, are striking exaggerated girlish poses. Several other kids in line are snickering.*)

RICK   Are they doing it again? I am so sick of that.

DELORES   Hey, they don't have any class at all. Stay away from them. I've seen them pick on other kids.

RICK   Yeah. Okay.

After school, as students are exiting campus, RICK has stayed behind a few minutes to help the art teacher put the room in order. He leaves by himself, but in a deserted corridor, HARRY and PETER are waiting for him. His only way out is past them.

HARRY (*to Peter*)   Here he comes. I wonder if he's wearing his Speedos under those jeans. Should we check it out?

PETER   What are you talking about? He'll think we want him to be our boyfriend. No, we need to teach him a lesson.

HARRY   Hey, I didn't mean it like that. (*to RICK*) Well, if it isn't the pervert. Hi, pervert. (*He begins to prance around.*)

RICK (*trying to push past them*)   You get a buzz out of belittling others, don't you? Just leave me alone. I haven't done anything to hurt you.

PETER   No, except gross me out. (*He grabs RICK's jacket and yanks him around.*) I can't stand the thought of you messing with little boys.

RICK (*steadying himself*)   I don't do that.

HARRY   That's not what we heard. You're too fruity for this school. (*He smacks RICK hard in the face with a closed fist. RICK's nose begins to bleed.*)

RICK (*taking a few steps back and touching his nose*)   You're sick!

PETER   Get that, Harry, the pervert is calling *you* sick. (*He rushes RICK and knocks him to the floor. Both HARRY and PETER begin kicking him. RICK tries to protect his head and face with his arms.*) Pervert! (*DELORES rounds the corner and sees what's going on.*)

DELORES   No! Stop that! Leave him alone! Somebody get security! (*The SECURITY GUARD rounds the corner and begins to yell as he races up to them.*)

SECURITY GUARD   Stop that right now! (*He grabs HARRY and PETER each by an arm and begins to hustle them away down the hall.*)

DELORES (*Races up to RICK and bends down to try to help him up.*)   Oh, my God. Are you okay?

PETER (*looking back over his shoulder at RICK*)   Hey, pervert, the Bible says guys like you will go to hell! And Delores, find a real man!

RICK (*RICK begins to get up, but he's a bit dazed, to DELORES.*)   Who made *them* God?

DELORES   Oh, your nose is bleeding. I don't even have a tissue.

RICK   I've got some in my backpack. Look under where my skateboard is sticking out. They threw it over against the wall.

SECURITY GUARD (*Before he turns the corner out of sight, he calls back.*)   Just wait there. I'll be right back. (*DELORES goes to retrieve the tissues.*)

RICK (*finally standing and rubbing his head*)   And those punks think I should go to hell. They don't even know me.

Discussion

1. Has Rick done anything to provoke an attack from Harry and Peter? Explain.
2. Where do you think Harry and Peter learned to name-call and attack someone that they believe is a homosexual?
3. What should be the consequences for Harry and Peter for their assault on Rick? How could they learn to treat Rick humanely?
4. Who else besides Rick will be hurt by this attack?
5. If you were Rick's parents, how would you react to your son being beat up at school?
6. If Rick is gay, where could he find help to understand and accept himself?
7. If you were to witness others belittling or attacking someone, what would you do?

This Is Our Bathroom

CHARACTERS
    VICTOR, SYLVIA, NANCY, KEISHA, LORRAINE, MR. O'CONNER, MOM

It is passing period between classes. VICTOR and his girlfriend, SYLVIA, are walking along the corridor.

VICTOR   So how was drama class? I bet you knocked them dead.

SYLVIA   I wish. But all we did was discuss how to personalize lines. We haven't even gotten any parts yet.

NANCY (*Approaches from opposite direction with KEISHA and LORRAINE, loudly.*)   Hey, look, you guys, it's miss movie star.

KEISHA   She wishes. She really thinks she's something.

LORRAINE   But we can fix that, can't we girls? (*The three pass by, then stop and laugh loudly as VICTOR and SYLVIA continue on their way.*)

VICTOR   What was that all about? Do you know those girls?

SYLVIA   Not really. And I don't think I want to. But I hope they're just trying to let me know to respect them, because I'm new here. I bet they're friends with each other from way back.

VICTOR   Why would anybody respect them if they act like that? I don't like this. They better not mess with you.

SYLVIA (*turning into class*)   Vic, don't worry about it. They're just blowing off steam. I'll see you at lunch, okay?

VICTOR   Okay, but watch your back.

At the beginning of lunch period, SYLVIA enters the girls' restroom. Inside are NANCY, KEISHA, and LORRAINE, smoking cigarettes and laughing.

NANCY   Well, look who's here. Hey, girl, you lost?

KEISHA (*giving SYLVIA a shove against the wall*)   You're in the wrong place, and I'd like to help you out. The door's that way.

SYLVIA   Hey, get your hands off me. (*She stands up straight and faces the three.*) Get out of my face. I have a right to use the bathroom.

LORRAINE   You don't get it, do you? And you sure don't diss us. And we decide who uses this bathroom and who doesn't, and you don't. (*She pushes SYLVIA back against the wall.*)

SYLVIA   Please, just leave me alone.

NANCY   Hey, don't tell us what to do. You don't have any respect, do you? Maybe you need us to teach you some of the rules around here. (*She yanks on SYLVIA's hair.*) You don't have lice, do you? (*She lets go of SYLVIA's hair and steps back. SYLVIA just stares at them.*)

KEISHA   Yeah, and I don't like how you dress, either. College girl stuff doesn't go around here. It looks stuck up. You're nobody.

LORRAINE   So you better stay out of our way. And this is our bathroom. Never come in here again if you know what's good for you. Come on, you guys, let's get her out of here. (*They grab SYLVIA by the arms and shove her mightily out the door. She struggles to catch her step, but sprawls out in the hall. Several students step around her, and some laugh. She struggles to her feet, tries to smooth out her hair and begins walking to lunch. She fights back tears.)*

VICTOR is sitting at a lunch table waiting for her. He sees SYLVIA approaching and can tell something is wrong. He rises and approaches.

VICTOR   My God, Sylvia, what happened?

SYLVIA   I'm so mad I could really hurt somebody! *(She slumps down at a table.)*

VICTOR *(Sits down beside her, puts his arm across her shoulders and tries to comfort her.)*   What is it? You look all messed up. What happened to your hair? There's a scratch on your cheek.

SYLVIA   Well, I didn't fall down on purpose, if that's what you're thinking. You remember those girls who made remarks about me in the hall this morning?

VICTOR   Yeah, two of them were in my last class. What happened? Did they do something to you?

SYLVIA   All I tried to do was use the bathroom. They were in there and began to shove me around. They said it was *their* bathroom. Then they shoved me into the hall and I fell.

VICTOR   So, you didn't watch your back like I said, did you? I'm so sorry. There are unwritten rules around here. Some kids control certain bathrooms, some control certain tables in the lunch area, some hang out in the quad area. You learn where to go after a while. I would have told you, but I'm not sure how the girl groups do it around here.

SYLVIA   So what am I supposed to do if I have to go to the bathroom? That's not fair. This school is for everyone. How dare they tell people where they can't go? *(She shakes her head.)* I should have stayed with my dad. I knew everybody in my old school. This place sucks.

VICTOR   Hey, it's not so bad after you learn your way around.

SYLVIA is holed up in her room when her MOM comes in and asks why she doesn't want dinner.

MOM   Sylvia, I fixed chicken. Come on. What's wrong?

SYLVIA   Mom, I love you, and I love being here with you, but I wish I could go back and live with Dad. I don't like this school.

MOM   But I thought you'd already made some friends. That guy Victor keeps calling and leaving messages on the machine. I wish you'd return his call. I thought he was a really nice guy.

SYLVIA   He is, Mom, and I love the drama class, but the other kids are rude.

MOM   Rude? How's that?

SYLVIA   Well, they think they own the place. The have little groups that hang out together.

MOM   That sounds normal to me. You just have to give it some time to get to know more people around there.

SYLVIA   Mom, it's hard to get to know kids who shove you around.

MOM   Shove you around! What are you talking about? You mean kids shoved you around?

SYLVIA *(beginning to cry)*   Mom, it was awful. And I'm crying because I'm so blasted mad. There were three of them, and they told me I couldn't use their bathroom, and that I was stuck up and that they needed to teach me a lesson, and they don't like the way I dress, and they messed up my hair, and then all three of them threw me out in the hall and I fell down and some kids laughed.

MOM *(hugging her)*   Oh, my God. That's awful. Did you tell anyone?

SYLVIA   I just told Victor. He said it's that way all over, and once you learn the ropes, you can avoid messes like that.

MOM   Learn the ropes?! Now that makes me really mad. I send my daughter to school to get an education, and she can't even use the restroom in peace! I don't think so.

SYLVIA   Mom, it's not worth a big old fuss. If I reported it, then they'd really have it in for me. I just think I'd be better off back with Dad.

MOM   No. No. We won't run away from this. I work hard and pay taxes so my kid can get an education, and I'm not going to stand by and have my daughter roughed up at school by some punks. I'll call in sick tomorrow and go down there with you and we'll see about this.

SYLVIA   Oh, Mom, please.

SYLVIA and MOM are seated in MR. O'CONNER's office.

MR. O'CONNER (*to SYLVIA's MOM*)   So, you look just like your daughter. We hope she's adjusting and enjoying being a student at our school. But what brings you in to see me this morning?

MOM   Well, I'm a little upset. You see, Sylvia was roughed up by some punks when she tried to use the restroom yesterday before lunch. She says different groups of kids have their own territories all over this campus. What's going on here?

MR. O'CONNER   Uh-oh. I'm sorry to hear that. Sylvia, this is the first I've heard of it. I wish you'd come right to me to let me know what happened then. But tell me about it. (*He takes out a notebook and begins to write.*)

Discussion

1. Why do you think kids tend to group together in certain ways by race, neighborhood, gang, and so forth?
2. Why do you think Nancy, Keisha, and Lorraine wanted to pick on Sylvia?
3. Do you think Sylvia should tell Mr. O'Conner who the girls were? Why or why not?
4. Would you want your mother to step in and try to put a stop to a situation like this? Why or why not?
5. How do you think the three girls should be punished?
6. If you were the counselor, what do you think would be the best way to solve the problem of groups excluding others from certain places on the campus?
7. If you were in charge, how do you think respect could be created between the four girls?

PART III: SEX VS. LOVE — CLEARING UP THE CONFUSION

Sending mixed signals

Hot Stuff

CHARACTERS
DARLA, LORIE, ANGELA, BRYCE, SETH, ABLE

LORIE and ANGELA are at a sleepover at DARLA's house.

DARLA   How come you broke up with Bryce, Lorie?

LORIE (*giggles*)   Oh, he's just out of it, if you know what I mean.

ANGELA   Really? I don't get what you mean by that. He's really smart. I think brains are sexy.

LORIE   Well, you can go for the brains if you want. Right now, I'm into instant gratification.

DARLA   Like instant what? He *does* have his own car. And he's got nice straight teeth.

LORIE   Well, he has a flat butt. And narrow shoulders. And he's a dud kisser.

ANGELA   So, you judge a guy by body parts? Hey, you can't judge a book by its cover.

DARLA   So what's a dud kisser?

LORIE   I don't know how to describe it. They've either got it or they don't. He doesn't know what to do with his tongue.

ANGELA   You could tell him what you like. How is he supposed to read your mind?

LORIE   If I have to tell them, I don't want them. Besides, he's little, if you know what I mean.

DARLA   Little? You went that far?

LORIE   Well, he doesn't look like much, but I thought I'd see if he had hidden talents. He doesn't.

ANGELA   So, did you do it with him?

LORIE   Wouldn't *you* like to know? But I will tell you this. Don't waste your time. He's only got a two-inch fuse. (*They all laugh.*)

ANGELA   Lorie, you're pitiful. You're a regular black widow who just uses up guys for their bodies. I hope Bryce never hears what you've been saying about him. He can't help what kind of body he's got. And I still think he's really fun to be around. He's got good manners, too.

LORIE   Well, life's short. I can't waste my time on geeks.

DARLA   Everybody to their own taste, I guess, but my dad says that girls should marry smart geeks because they're the ones that will make all the money.

ANGELA   You guys are so immature. You both deserve guys who just want girls for their bodies and to cook and clean.

LORIE   Well, hey, so far, there are plenty of guys around that are into bodies. (*She admires herself in the mirror.*) I like choice and variety. Let the good times roll.

DARLA   If I looked as good as you do, Lorie, I might feel the same way. But I really hope some guy will love me for who I am, you know, be my best friend, and be able to overlook my faults.

ANGELA   That sounds good. My dad says that there are a lot of decent guys out there, but you have to grow up a little bit to recognize them. Besides, size isn't everything. My mom says, "It's not the size of the ship. It's the motion of the ocean." Who a guy is is a lot more important than all the physical appearance stuff. But I wish guys felt the same way about girls.

LORIE   You guys are getting on my nerves. It's time to pig out and watch the movie I brought. Where are the chips?

BRYCE, SETH, and ABLE are in the garage working on BRYCE's car.

SETH   How come you broke up with Lorie, Bryce? She is one good-looking woman!

BRYCE   Well, we've got different ideas about things.

ABLE   What do different ideas matter with a hot girl like Lorie? If she's giving it away, I say take it.

SETH   Yeah. I hear guys say she likes to do all kinds of crazy things.

ABLE   You know, like on some of those adult channels on TV.

BRYCE (*looking up from the engine*)   Yeah. That was part of the problem. I felt like I was just a piece of meat.

SETH (*laughing*)   My grandpa says that girls never acted like that in his time.

ABLE   Well, some guys like that. As long as they don't spread disease, of course. I heard she gave some guy the drip.

BRYCE   Never mind, of course, that somebody gave it to her once. But I will say, she's too racy for me.

SETH   What's the matter, man? Don't you get horny?

BRYCE (*frowning at SETH*)   Of course I do. I'm normal, and healthy, but I get put off by a girl who goes for the jugular. I'd like to get to know someone. You know, really care about them.

ABLE   Don't you like it when they wear those sexy, tight clothes?

BRYCE   Yeah. I look, but I wouldn't want my girlfriend dressing like that.

SETH   Why not, man? Being seen with a babe like that would make everyone think you were a real stud.

ABLE   Yeah, I love it when I go to a party and they're showing off their goods. And then they dance a little, and everything moves. Oh, yeah!

BRYCE   Hey, but you just see them as sex objects.

SETH   So? That's why they dress that way. I like big chests and nice butts. I say if they want to put it out there, I'll look.

BRYCE   What if a girl isn't so good looking? Is she just dog meat?

SETH   Hey, life is hard. Survival of the fittest. No scrawny ugly women for me. But I wouldn't want anybody thinking about my sister like that.

ABLE   Well, right now, I'll go for the good body parts. I'll worry about personality and being nice and stuff like that later. So maybe I'll give Lorie a call. You won't mind, will you, man?

BRYCE   No, she's all yours. But Seth, do you suppose you could set me up with your sister Angela? I'd like to get to know her.

SETH   No problem, man. I guess she'd be safe with you. I won't let her see some guy who would dehumanize her.

ABLE   Great logic, man. It's okay for you to go for girls as meat, but treat your sister like a princess, right? What's wrong with this picture?

Discussion

1. What qualities do you think are needed for a true, loving relationship between partners?
2. Is sex the same as love? Explain.
3. Do you think guys really respect Lorie as a person, or are they just using her for sexual gratification?
4. Do you think Lorie will ever find a fulfilling, true love relationship? Explain.
5. Are a hot body and clever sexual technique necessary for a fulfilling relationship? Explain.
6. How would you feel if you believed people were judging your worth as a person by your body parts and sexual technique?

If You've Got It, Flaunt It

CHARACTERS
ELAINE, MARIE, HEATHER, WES, ZACK, MOM

ELAINE, MARIE, and HEATHER are in the girls' gym dressing for class after physical education.

ELAINE   I hate getting all sweaty like this, but I love volleyball. I wish we had time for a decent shower.

MARIE   Well, nobody'll know you're sweaty with the baggy clothes you wear.

ELAINE   Hey, they're comfortable. And I don't want those guys in history class undressing me with their eyes. They're so blatant.

HEATHER (*slipping on a low cut tank top*)   Oh, it won't hurt them to get a few looks. That's probably all they get anyway.

MARIE   Heather, you're so cold-blooded. Don't you get cold with that skimpy top on? And that skirt? Man, my mom would kill me if she even thought I was wearing something like that to school.

HEATHER   If I like it, that's what counts. I like having guys admire me. I'll only be young once. You know, that girl in third period who had the baby, have you seen how fat she still is? She even has stretch marks on her hips.

ELAINE   Yes, I know her. She's really nice.

MARIE   Yeah, she's a good student, too.

HEATHER   So? You don't see guys swarming around her now, do you?

ELAINE   No. Maybe that's not what she wants.

MARIE   Well, my mom says guys in high school are still so busy wondering if all their parts work, if you know what I mean, that they'll come on to a post. (*They all laugh.*)

HEATHER   Hey, that's their problem. Zack loves it when guys look at me.

ELAINE   No offense intended, but why do you think that is? Does he want the other guys to think that he's the big stud because he's got the girl they all lust after? That doesn't sound like a healthy relationship to me.

HEATHER   Well, thank you very much, miss athlete, with your sweat shirt and gym shoes. I haven't noticed any guys standing in line for you. Hey, if you've got it, flaunt it! That's what my mom says.

MARIE   Hey, hey, cool it, you guys. This conversation is getting toxic. It's a free country.

MARIE and ELAINE exit, but HEATHER goes to the mirror, touches up her make-up, then turns back and forth admiring herself. She tucks her tank top in, pulling it tight and low. She exits. Later that evening, ELAINE is at home talking to MOM.

ELAINE   Mom, can I talk to you about something?

MOM   Sure, honey. Did something happen at school today?

ELAINE   Nothing serious, Mom. It's just that, you know, I dress kinda dumpy. Sweats all the time.

MOM   Honey, you're at school for business. And they're comfortable aren't they? Did something happen?

ELAINE   Oh, this girl in gym class, Heather. She's very pretty, and she dresses so that not much is left to the imagination. You get my drift?

MOM   So?

ELAINE   Well, she says that's how to attract guys. And it really works for her. All I get noticing me is some geeky guy who wants to tell me dud jokes. Do you think you could help me, you know, spice it up a bit?

MOM   Sure, if you think that's what you want. But in good taste, of course. Guys are attracted to pretty women. You're a beautiful young woman. You have nothing to be ashamed of. Some guys prefer the natural type, like you. To start, you could wear something besides baggy sweats.

ELAINE   But I don't want guys just looking at my chest, like they do Heather.

MOM   No, of course not. If you show too much, they can't help thinking of sex. It's just natural for them. They don't think about who you really are, your personality, talents, character. And for some of them, they think if you show off too much, it's okay to grab, or make crude remarks.

ELAINE   I get it, Mom. Thanks. So can I go shopping this weekend? I think I can get a few trendy things without being trashy.

HEATHER and ZACK are kicking back at his friend's apartment.

ZACK   You look really good, today, baby. I love it when all those goobers look at you and foam at the mouth.

HEATHER (*giggles*)   That's good. You don't think this tank top is too low?

ZACK   No, baby. It just proves you're all there. I love it. (*He grabs her and pushes her down on the couch.*)

HEATHER   Zack, please. Not now.

ZACK   Why not? I'm in the mood. You turn me on.

HEATHER   You act like you just want me for my body. You and your horny friends. (*She shoves him away, stands up, adjusts her clothes.*) You know, I'm a real person, too.

ZACK   Are you gonna be all up tight? That's not fair. You look like you do, then you get all prissy on me. What's the matter with you? You tease, but you don't wanna please. That makes me mad! (*He gets up and glares at her.*) Get your jacket. I'm taking you home.

HEATHER   Zack, please. What did I do?

WES sits at the computer between ELAINE and MARIE in the computer lab.

MARIE   Hi, Wes. What's up?

WES   Oh, I just wanted to absorb your awesome essence.

ELAINE   Wow! Where'd you get that? Sounds like you've been reading too much poetry.

WES   Well, I can't help that. But you ladies might need some help on the computer lesson. We're getting into the really sophisticated stuff now. And I am the teacher's aide. (*He gives a grand gesture.*) Besides, you're doing great in volleyball. Some serve you've got there, Elaine.

ELAINE   You noticed that, huh?

WES (*laughs*)   Hey, yeah. A man appreciates natural beauties like yourselves, not to mention your grace and skill.

MARIE   That's really nice of you to say, Wes. I thought you were just a quiet little twerp who still looked at Playboy in his tree fort. (*They all laugh.*)

WES   Hey, a gentleman can be classy, but that doesn't mean he's dead. (*pause*) Anyway, we better get into this lesson. But would you guys like to review this information over hamburgers after school? I can treat this time, but the next time's on you. (*The girls smile and nod.*)

ELAINE   That sounds cool, Wes. You know, you're a lot different than I first thought.

MARIE   Yeah, you're smart and funny.

WES   Cool. Thanks for noticing. My dad always says you can't tell a book by its cover.

Discussion

1. How much can you tell about a person from your first impression?
2. How much does appearance bear on someone's ability to be a satisfying, loving companion?
3. Heather wants to be liked by dressing provocatively. How is it working?
4. What influences affect how young people dress?
5. Can girls dress in revealing clothes without having boys first respond to them at a sexual level? When, if ever, is it appropriate for girls to dress in sexually provocative clothing?
6. Do you think Heather understands why so many guys want to hang around her? Do they really want to be her friends?
7. What does "dressing in good taste" mean?
8. How can Heather change her image of being a sex symbol to the boys, to that of being a complete person?

Being used

Skit 34

Whatsa Matter? Are You Gay?

CHARACTERS
  SEAN, MELINDA, YVETTE, OSCAR

On a warm summer evening, the four are lounging around MELINDA's house. They are in and out of the pool, listening to music, and SEAN has brought a fifth of vodka.

MELINDA   Hey, Sean, no glass over by the pool. Even if my folks are in Las Vegas, I'll follow that rule.

SEAN   Okay, okay, I'll use the plastic cups. That make you happy? But, turn up the music, will you? Yvette, why don't you step this way? (*He makes a grandiose bow.*) This man wants to dance.

YVETTE (*rising and approaching him*)   You know, you're a real drama queen.

OSCAR (*to MELINDA*)   You hear that? I knew it. He's a queen.

SEAN (*dancing with YVETTE*)   Well, some people here know I'm not a queen. Don't they, woman? (*He pulls her close.*)

YVETTE   Well, you don't need to prove it right now. Ease up. (*They continue to dance.*)

MELINDA (*approaching OSCAR*)   Come on, Oscar. Dance with me. I gotta move around a little or I'll get cold with this wet suit on.

OSCAR (*Rises and begins to dance with her.*)   Thanks. Don't mind if I do.

MELINDA   Mmm. What's that scent you're wearing? It turns me on. (*She pulls him close.*)

OSCAR (*They dance, holding each other close.*)   "Obsession." I guess girls like it, huh?

MELINDA   Oh, yes. By the way, are you still going out with Kerrie? I haven't seen you with her lately.

OSCAR   You noticed, huh? Yeah, she and I didn't see eye to eye.

MELINDA   Wow. You're even a poet. (*Laughs and gives him a hug.*) I wondered why you came over here with Sean if you were still tight with her. But you don't see me complaining.

OSCAR   Yeah, my mom said I needed to get out more. (*pause*) Say, are you getting thirsty?

MELINDA   I could use a refresher. (*They move to the patio bar and she pours them both another drink.*)

OSCAR   Whoa, girl, ease up on the vodka. I don't want to get too silly.

MELINDA   Relax. We're just getting rid of our inhibitions. That's what the health teacher said happens when alcohol messes with your nervous system. But, I'll watch out for you.

OSCAR   Cool. A guy always likes to be watched out for. (*They sit down on lounge chairs.*)

MELINDA   Hey, are you shivering? You want a sweatshirt or something?

OSCAR (*sipping from his drink*)   That'd be good.

MELINDA   Come on. I've got a really big one in my closet. (*They rise and go into the house. The other two have gone back into the pool.*)

OSCAR   Uh-oh. The woman is hauling me into her bedroom.

MELINDA (*Sliding open her closet door, she yanks a sweatshirt off a hook.*)   Here it is. (*She turns, holds it out, and sees OSCAR shivering.*) Oooh, you look cold. (*She steps to him to hand him the shirt, but then, she reaches around in back of him and pulls him close.*) Mmm. Nice.

OSCAR (*Steps back.*)   Hey, I'm sorry. I think the liquor is messing up my thinking.

MELINDA (*stepping up to him and kissing him*)   Do you see me complaining? Why do you think I dragged you in my bedroom?

OSCAR (*pulling back*)   Wait a minute. Wait a minute. Don't get me wrong. This is nice, but—

MELINDA   But what? Come on. Nobody'll know. (*She pulls him close again.*)

OSCAR   You're tempting, but we don't even know each other.

MELINDA   So? Let's get acquainted. Come on.

OSCAR   Gosh, I'm feeling a little dizzy. I need some fresh air.

MELINDA   Want me to open the window? Come on. I can get you all warmed up.

OSCAR (*pulling away from her again*)   No. No. I can't do this. It's not right.

MELINDA (*sarcastically*)   Well, thank you very much. I thought guys appreciated getting some. Whatsa matter? Are you gay?

OSCAR (*embarrassed*)   Hey, I didn't mean to offend you. I just don't want to be physical with someone when I don't even really know them.

MELINDA   Yeah, sure. Thanks a lot. Oh, hey, I think your ride's here. Maybe you better go, Cinderella! (*She points toward the bedroom door; they exit.*)

After school, OSCAR and SEAN are sitting in SEAN's car waiting for YVETTE to give a ride home.

SEAN   So, how did you like Melinda? Do I have good taste in women, or what?

OSCAR   She's good looking, all right.

SEAN   Yeah, and she knows how to make guys happy. So, did you score?

OSCAR   Hey, it's not a game.

SEAN   Game? What are you talking about? If girls want to give it away, a guy is a chump if he doesn't take it.

OSCAR   Yeah, that's what I hear.

SEAN   Well?

OSCAR   No.

SEAN   Why not? I told her when I brought you over that you had just broken up with someone. I told her you were hot. She was really looking forward to meeting you.

OSCAR   Well, we met. Thank you. But a gentleman never tells, even if he did "score."

SEAN   When I saw her in class today, she didn't smile much. Just said you were okay, but not to bring you over there anymore. You didn't insult her, I hope.

OSCAR   I didn't mean to, but she got kinda mad. Hey, I gotta love someone first.

SEAN   Gee, you are really old-fashioned, you know that?

YVETTE (*approaching, then climbing in back seat*)   Hi, you guys. Thanks for waiting. (*to OSCAR*) By the way, what happened between you and Melinda? Her feelings are really hurt.

OSCAR   I'm sorry to hear that. She's just not my type, I guess.

YVETTE   But what did you do to make her all upset?

OSCAR   Nothing. She made herself all upset. Why can't a guy say "no"?

Discussion

1. Why do Melinda, Sean, and Yvette think Oscar is odd?
2. Where do you think they got their idea that casual sex is normal?
3. How might the use of alcohol lead to unplanned sex?
4. Where do you think Oscar got his idea that he wanted sex to be special with someone he loves?
5. What physical dangers might be associated with casual sex? What emotional problems could be associated with casual sex?
6. Can young people love each other romantically without having sex? What might be the advantages of waiting to have sex until both partners are mature and independent?
7. If you were a counselor, what would you tell young people about safe limits for romantic relationships?

You Would If You Loved Me

CHARACTERS

NICOLE, BRYAN, CELESTE, KEITH

It's Friday night. NICOLE, BRYAN, CELESTE, and KEITH are just leaving a teen dance club at l2:30 a.m. BRYAN is driving his van.

BRYAN   Okay, you guys, I'm going to drive by the lake. We can stop and enjoy the full moon for a while. Any objections?

KEITH   Sounds cool to me. Celeste, your mom won't care if you're a little past curfew, will she?

CELESTE (*cuddling up to him in the back seat*)   I don't think so. She likes you. She thinks you're smart and will make lots of money. But she doesn't know everything, thank goodness. (*giggles*)

KEITH   Don't listen to her, you guys. I'm innocent. Honest. (*They all laugh.*)

NICOLE (*a little nervous*)   Gee, the lake's out of the way, isn't it? Do you have enough gas?

BRYAN   Hey, babe, I take care of business. Don't worry. You're safe with me.

NICOLE   I didn't mean to offend you, Bryan. And I don't want to be a wet blanket, but I really am kind of tired. I have to go to work at ten tomorrow.

BRYAN (*turning on her*)   You want to waste a night like this? Come on now.

NICOLE   We already had a good time. But if we don't stay there too long … .

BRYAN   Don't sweat it. (*He turns the van into the parking lot beside the lake.*) Here we are. (*to Nicole*) Come on. I've got a blanket in the back. Let's go down by the water and relax a while. (*motioning toward CELESTE and KEITH*) I think they want to be alone. Bring the wine cooler, will you? (*He gets the blanket from the back and they go down on the beach, spread the blanket out, and sit down.*)

NICOLE (*sipping wine from a cup*)   Gosh, it is a beautiful night. It would be a shame not to enjoy this.

BRYAN   That's a girl. (*He kisses her. NICOLE drinks more wine.*)

NICOLE   I wonder how warm the water is? (*She kicks off her sandals and rises, heads for the water.*)

BRYAN (*They wade and splash around a little.*)   Oh, you're getting cold. (*He embraces her.*)

NICOLE   Yeah, I better dry off. What time is it anyway?

BRYAN   We haven't been here that long. Come on, let's go relax a little more. You need to get warmed up.

NICOLE   Well, the wine is making me feel relaxed. Maybe for a few minutes. (*Once they sit on the blanket again, BRYAN eases her down, kisses her again, and begins to put his hands on her. She squirms away.*) Bryan! Please. No.

BRYAN   Oh, come on. We shouldn't waste a night like this. We'll only be young once.

NICOLE   No, Bryan. We talked about this. No.

BRYAN (*getting irritated*)   I can't understand you. What's the big deal? Everybody does it. It's natural. What are you holding out for anyway?

NICOLE   I don't want to argue with you about it. You know I care about you. Don't get mad. I'm just not ready.

BRYAN   Well, you got me all turned on, and now you want to be a cold fish. I don't get it. You said you loved me. That's what people do when they love each other. If something happens, I'll be there for you. I even have a condom. You'll be safe.

NICOLE   You know you turn me on too. And I do love you. But I thought when people really love each other, they want what's best for each other.

BRYAN   Hey, that's what making love is, doing what's best for each other.

NICOLE   But only when the time is right. It's right for you, I guess. Don't you care that it's not right for me?

BRYAN (*getting up and tucking in his shirt*)   Come on. Let's go. You gotta go to work tomorrow. I hope the others are finished. (*He pulls the blanket out from under her.*)

NICOLE   Finished? So you planned this all along, didn't you?

BRYAN   Think what you want. If a girl really loves a guy, she proves it.

Back in the van on the way home.

KEITH   I thought we'd have more time for a little walk around the lake. What was your hurry?

CELESTE   Yeah. I hate to have such a beautiful night end.

BRYAN   Nicole, here, is worried about getting to her job in the morning. She has trouble enjoying the good times.

NICOLE   Bryan, that's not fair.

BRYAN   Well, I've been fair long enough. (*They ride in silence a while. He pulls up in front of her house.*) Here you go, Nicole.

NICOLE   Okay. Thanks. See you tomorrow night?

BRYAN   No, Nicole. I plan to enjoy the rest of my life. You take care, now, hear? (*He guns his engine, and his tires squeal as he speeds away.*)

Monday at school, NICOLE meets CELESTE in the hall between classes.

CELESTE   Hey, Nicole. What happened between you and Bryan?

NICOLE   Oh, hi, Celeste. I didn't put out, so he got upset.

CELESTE   Oh. Some guys can be like that, I guess. I told Keith I wasn't ready to go all the way yet, and he whined around a while, but finally he said that he respected me for it. He said that maybe we could get to know each other as friends and find other things to do. In the van Friday, we were just talking and listening to music. I bet you thought that we were doing it, didn't you?

NICOLE   Well, Bryan made me think that's what you were doing.

CELESTE   He was trying to lay guilt, huh? Too bad. Some guys are just thinking of what they want.

NICOLE   Yeah. I really did like him, though. But I already saw him before school sweet-talking another girl. I'm glad I found out how much I mattered to him before I spent any more time with him.

CELESTE   But when the time is right with the right person, it's going to be great, huh?

NICOLE   You said it. And then it'll really mean something special.

Discussion

1.   Where do you think Bryan got his idea about sex being a natural thing that you just do if you feel like it?
2.   If Nicole had drunk more wine, how might that have affected whether she had sex or not?
3.   What do you think Celeste and Nicole mean when they talk about the right time and the right person with whom to have sex?
4.   What physical problems for either partner might be associated with casual, recreational sex?
5.   What emotional problems for either partner might be associated with recreational sex?
6.   Do you agree with Nicole when she says that if you really love someone, you want what is best for them?

Someone to Love

CHARACTERS

ELLEN, CODY, CECELIA, MOM

ELLEN and CODY are in her mom's apartment alone. MOM is gone on a trip with her boyfriend.

ELLEN   I don't know what I'd do if I didn't have you, Cody. It gets so lonesome around here, just me and Cecelia. I get bored trying to talk about things with a three-year-old.

CODY   Hey, you've got me. But listen, I've gotta get home. I've got a lot of homework. One of us has to graduate. Then I can try to get a job, and maybe we can get our own place.

ELLEN   I can hardly wait. I've gotta get out of here. I love Cecelia, but my mom depends on me to watch her. I guess she's trying to catch up on the good times she says she missed by having me when she was only fifteen.

CODY   Didn't your mom know about birth control?

ELLEN   I don't know. We never talk about stuff like that. I think she thinks I learn all that business at school.

CODY   Does your mom know you're on the pill?

ELLEN   Heck, no. I don't want her in my business. She just spends time talking to me about her troubles with her boyfriends. As if I'm some kind of a counselor.

CODY   Well, I like how you counsel me. (*They laugh.*) I haven't been tense for a long time. But Cecelia sure is nosy. Little kids don't know what's going on, do they?

ELLEN   She knows Mom's gone a lot. (*pause*) Actually, she knows more than a little kid should. (*thoughtfully*) And so do I.

CODY   Uh-oh. It's getting cloudy in here. (*Looks at his watch.*) Oops. Now I really gotta go. (*Kisses her good-bye and exits.*)

ELLEN   (*Peeks into CECELIA's bedroom.*)   You asleep, Cece? (*CECELIA is in her bed hugging her teddy bear.*)

CECELIA   No. I want Mama.

ELLEN   I'm sorry, Cece. She's not home yet. Maybe tomorrow. But I'm here. Can I have a hug? (*She hugs CECELIA, grabs a story book off the shelf, sits on the bed, snaps on the light.*) Here, let's read a story, okay?

CECELIA   Okay. (*She sits up.*) I want Cinderella.

ELLEN   Well, how about this one? This is about Babar, you know the one about the elephant.

CECELIA   No. I want Cinderella.

ELLEN   Okay. (*rising*) Where is it? (*CECELIA points to the shelf. ELLEN shuffles through books till she finds it.*) Here it is! (*Sits and begins to read.*) "Once upon a time, there was a young girl named Cinderella." (*She reads on until CECELIA nods off clutching her teddy bear, then she turns out the light and tiptoes out.*) So, here I am, by myself again. I really do need my own life.

A couple of weeks later, ELLEN confronts her MOM.

ELLEN   Mom, I've got to talk to you. (*MOM glances up from the TV.*) Uh, you know Cody and I want to get our own place.

MOM   Well, that's a stupid idea. (*Mutes the TV.*) Who's going to pay for it? He isn't even graduated from high school yet. Can't you find a real man to take care of you? (*Turns the TV back up to full volume.*) Besides, I need you to help me around here. And Cecelia loves you.

ELLEN   Mom, turn that thing down, please! (*MOM mutes the TV.*)

MOM   Well, what is it? This is my favorite program. I missed it last week.

ELLEN   Mom, I missed my period.

MOM (*loudly*)   What? (*She rises and stands in front of ELLEN.*) What's been going on around here? I can't trust you to leave you in charge for a few days without you giving it up to some boy?

ELLEN   Mom, please! I don't know if I'm just late from stress, or what, but if I am pregnant, I figured I better let you know.

MOM   Gee, thanks a lot. You just made my day. So who is the creep, that bum Cody?

ELLEN   Mom, please. I really like him.

MOM   Like? Like? So if you *like* a boy, it's okay to have sex, just like grownups? (*pause*) So you think because you're almost sixteen, you're all grown up? (*She sits down and turns her back on ELLEN.*)

ELLEN   Yeah, Mom. Just the age you were when you got pregnant. But this baby is going to have a mom who loves her and stays with her and doesn't farm her out to an older sister every time the mom feels like playing.

MOM (*Rises, stalks over to ELLEN, and slaps her across the face.*)   Don't you ever talk to your mom like that again! I gave you life. I deserve respect.

ELLEN (*Turns away crying.*)   So do I, Mom. And I need someone to love. Even if Cody can't take care of me yet, I'll have my baby to love.

MOM (*softening, then trying to hug ELLEN*)   Oh, honey, I'm so sorry. I didn't mean to hit you. Why didn't you tell me you were so lonesome? You should have told me.

ELLEN   Mom, I tried. I know you love me. I'm sorry.

MOM   So is Cody the father? (*ELLEN nods.*) That figures. Didn't you know enough to use protection? I would have gotten you anything you needed.

ELLEN   Mom, I got on the pill myself at the health department. But I quit taking them.

MOM   Well, that was a stupid thing to do.

ELLEN   Mom, please don't call me stupid. Cody really cares for me. I know we're too young. He doesn't know I quit taking them. I just thought that it would happen if it was meant to, and if we had our own baby to love, maybe we could be a real family.

Discussion

1.   Do you think Ellen became pregnant on purpose? Why?
2.   How do you think Cody will respond when he finds out?
3.   What problems will he face as a teen father not yet graduated from high school?
4.   Do you think Ellen will ever become a high school graduate? How can she manage to finish school as a teen mother?
5.   If Cody and Ellen get their own place, how will they support themselves and their baby?
6.   What kind of place will they be able to afford?
7.   Now that Ellen is pregnant, should Cody and Ellen get married? What would be the advantage to them of being married?
8.   What impact would their being married have on their child as it grows up?
9.   If you were Ellen's counselor and she told you she was lonely, was tired of taking over her mother's responsibilities, and was having trouble finishing her education, how would you advise her?

In the danger zone

I Know He Loves Me

CHARACTERS
NEAL, MAGGIE, JANETTE, ADAM, ANDREW

NEAL and MAGGIE are sitting in his car in the school parking lot before classes begin.

NEAL   You know how much I love you, baby. You know I need you. So please don't wear those jeans again. Guys look at you. I can't stand that.

MAGGIE   Neal, my mom bought me these jeans. They're stretch, so they fit good. I can't help it if guys look at me. You know I love you, so mellow out.

NEAL (*He frowns.*)   I try. I really do, but if I lost you, I don't know what I'd do. Would you please let your t-shirt hang out?

MAGGIE   Oh, please. That looks sloppy. I am wearing the earrings you gave me. I love them. I know they cost you a bunch. (*She touches her ear and fingers the gold hoop.*) Well, it's almost time for class. I better go. (*She starts to open the car door.*)

NEAL (*grabbing her arm*)   No, wait. Show me you love me before you go.

MAGGIE (*leaning over to give him a little kiss*)   You know I love you. (*NEAL pulls her across the seat and tries to give her a long, hard kiss, but she pulls away.*) Neal, please. Not here. Kids are walking by.

NEAL (*squeezing her arm hard enough to give her a bruise*)   So what? I want them to know how much I love you.

MAGGIE   Neal, let go. That hurts.

NEAL (*Shoves her away.*)   Get out then.

MAGGIE (*getting out and shutting the door carefully*)   Sorry, Neal. See you at lunch, okay?

NEAL (*getting out and slamming the door*)   Maybe.

JANETTE approaches across the parking lot and calls to MAGGIE.

JANETTE   Maggie, wait up.

MAGGIE   Oh, hi, Janette.

JANETTE   Did I just see Neal slamming his car door and storming off? What's up with him?

MAGGIE (*She wipes at her eyes.*)   Oh, he's just in another one of his moods. I guess I made him mad again.

JANETTE   Gee, he's really touchy, isn't he? What is it this time?

MAGGIE   He doesn't like these jeans. He thinks other guys look at me. He says he loves me too much.

JANETTE   But if he loves you so much, how come he makes you cry? I don't get it.

MAGGIE   He says I'm his whole life. I've never had a guy care about me so much before.

JANETTE   Yeah, I hear that. And those gold earrings are awesome. Hey, it's none of my business. But I wish you'd come over to my house tonight to study for the chemistry test. A few other kids will be there. We're gonna get some pizza and try to ease the pain of cramming. Hey, Neal can come too, if he wants. Adam will be there, so it won't be all girls.

MAGGIE   That sounds really cool. Let me think about it. I'll let you know at lunch, okay? I'll ask Neal and see what he thinks.

JANETTE   Ask him? Ask him? I just meant he could come if you wanted him to, not that you'd have to ask his permission for you to come.

MAGGIE   He doesn't like me going out where other guys are. Sorry. It's easier if I can talk him into things first.

JANETTE   Shoot, Adam and I discuss things, but I don't have to ask his permission for anything. I don't think I could stand that.

MAGGIE   Yeah, well, I guess he's afraid of something happening to me.

JANETTE   Hey, it's your life. But I hope I see you tonight. We're meeting about seven.

JANETTE, MAGGIE, ADAM, ANDREW, and two other students are seated around the kitchen table at JANETTE's house. Textbooks and notebooks, pizza, and soft drinks are scattered around the table.

ADAM   So, Maggie, is Neal coming over or not?

MAGGIE   No. Actually, I didn't even tell him I was coming. I didn't feel like trying to explain to him that we're all on the up and up. He's not taking chemistry this semester anyway.

JANETTE   Hmmm. Okay. We'll take good care of you.

They go over their notes and chapters for an hour. ANDREW is standing over MAGGIE pointing out some corrections she needs to make in her notes. NEAL knocks at the door.

JANETTE   I wonder who that is. Was anyone else coming?

ADAM   Not that I know of.

JANETTE (*opening the door*)   Neal. Oh, hi. Come on in. We're hot into studying for the chemistry test.

NEAL (*shoving her aside*)   Is Maggie here? (*He sees her at the table with ANDREW standing over her. His eyes grow dark with rage.*) There you are! Come on, we're going right now! (*He strides to her, grabs her arm, and yanks her out of her chair.*)

MAGGIE   Neal, let go of me! I just came over here to study. I thought you were going to help your cousin fix his car. Let go.

NEAL (*pushing her toward the door*)   I *told* you I didn't want you hanging out with other guys. So you sneak around behind my back. I had to find out from your mom that you were over here.

ANDREW (*striding toward NEAL*)   Hey, man. She said to let go of her. You don't own her.

NEAL (*Lets go of MAGGIE and turns on ANDREW.*)   Hey, punk! Stay away from her.

ANDREW   Listen, she's a free person. And you sure don't tell *me* what to do. (*to MAGGIE*) Get back. This guy's outta here. (*to ADAM*) Help me get his butt outta here.

ADAM (*grabbing NEAL's arm*)   Yeah. Outta here! You don't tell us what to do!

NEAL (*Takes a swing at ADAM. ANDREW jumps in and shoves NEAL toward the door.*)   Come on, Maggie. Come on!

MAGGIE (*Tries to get between them.*)   Come on, you guys. Stop it!

NEAL (*to MAGGIE*)   You tramp! I wouldn't have to be here if you hadn't been sneaking around. (*He tries to slap her face, but she turns away. His fingers catch a hoop earring and tear it from her ear.*)

ADAM   You slime! You hit a girl. (*He smacks NEAL in the mouth.*)

MAGGIE (*Backs up with her hand clamped to her bleeding ear.*)   My God, Neal. What's the matter with you?

NEAL (*Looks at her with an anguished expression.*)   Oh, my God. I'm so sorry. But I love you. Are you coming with me or not?

JANETTE   Maggie, don't go with a guy who hits you. You want me to call 911?

Discussion

1. What choices could Maggie make on how to handle this situation?
2. If she goes with Neal and continues the relationship, how is it likely to work out?
3. If she lets Janette call 911, what is likely to happen to their relationship? What is likely to happen to Neal?
4. Does Neal really love Maggie, or does he just need her? What is the difference?
5. What might have attracted Maggie to Neal?
6. If you were the school counselor, what kind of help could you recommend to Maggie to help her maintain healthy relationships in the future?
7. What kind of help would you recommend to Neal?

If I Can't Have You, Nobody Can

CHARACTERS
TAMARA (PAUL's jealous girlfriend), PAUL, SYBIL, YOLANDA, ANDY

ANDY, PAUL, and SYBIL are on the swim team. YOLANDA and TAMARA are waiting for them outside the locker rooms after swim practice.

TAMARA (*to YOLANDA*)   This shouldn't be taking him so long. That slut Sybil better not be in there coming on to him.

YOLANDA   Easy girl. Andy says nothing's going on to be suspicious about.

TAMARA   You know guys stick together on stuff like this. They make me sick. But I don't like how he looks at her.

YOLANDA   Here they come now. Uh-oh. He's walking with her. (*to TAMARA*) Don't get all upset now. Just be cool. It's probably nothing.

ANDY   Hi, you guys. Thanks for waiting, Yolanda. You want to go grab a hamburger?

YOLANDA   Sure. Gosh, you smell like chlorine.

ANDY   Yeah. I know. It means I'm pure, I guess. (*They laugh and she and ANDY exit.*)

TAMARA   Bye, you guys. (*She approaches PAUL and gets between him and SYBIL.*) What took you so long? (*Turns to SYBIL.*) What are you doing here? I thought girls' practice was on Tuesdays and Thursdays.

SYBIL (*frowning at her*)   I came in for some extra practice. Why do you care?

TAMARA   Don't act dumb, girl. You know Paul's my boyfriend. Take heed, if you know what's good for you.

PAUL   Gee, Tamara. Lighten up, will you?

TAMARA   Hey, I'm honest about how I feel, unlike some others I know.

PAUL   Can we talk about this some other time? I'm tired and hungry. (*Turns to SYBIL.*) You're really cutting your time on the freestyle. I bet we'll kick butt against the Tigers next week. Take care, now.

SYBIL   Thanks. The extra practice is paying off. See you. (*exits*)

TAMARA   You know she's a slut, don't you? She makes me sick!

PAUL   She seems okay to me. She's a really good swimmer. Why do you care, anyway?

TAMARA   Well, you spend more time at swim practice than you do with me.

PAUL   Sorry about that, but we're in the middle of the season. We can't slack off or we won't have a chance in the competition. Coach says to either do it well or forget it, because the other teams will kick our butts.

TAMARA   I guess. I just really get tired of waiting around for you all the time.

PAUL   You don't have to wait for me. I'm a big boy.

TAMARA   I know, but I get lonesome.

PAUL   Well, you could read a book, or something.

TAMARA   Gee, thanks.

During the next swim practice, PAUL has been coaching SYBIL on how to improve her starts.

PAUL   You're getting it. You got noticeably more distance on your entry that time. That was great.

SYBIL   That's good to hear. Your tips are really helping me. I appreciate it.

PAUL   Well, you're fun to help.

SYBIL (*laughs*)   But I wish I could do as well in algebra. Are you any good as a coach in that? I struggle to catch on. I guess that's why I'd rather be at swim practice. I feel like I make progress here.

PAUL   You need help in algebra? Yeah, I do okay in it. You want some extra help?

SYBIL   Oh, gosh, I'd hate to be a bother to anyone.

PAUL   No bother. You want to meet me at the branch library this evening and I'll help you if I can?

SYBIL   You would? Wow. That would be great. What time?

PAUL   Oh, how's 7:30? That would give us a couple of hours.

SYBIL   Super. I'll see you then. But hey, won't your girlfriend get mad?

PAUL   Don't worry about her. I'm going to break up with her anyway.

SYBIL   Not on my account, I hope.

PAUL   No, this has been coming on for a long time. She wants me to be with her all the time. That's not good for either one of us. In fact, I was planning to tell her tomorrow.

PAUL and TAMARA are seated on a bench in the park.

TAMARA   So, I gave you a break and got a book from the library. I didn't wait for you at swim practice. So why do you want to see me here?

PAUL   Well, you know I think you are a super person.

TAMARA   Uh-oh. I don't like how this is going.

PAUL   Well, I think I get on your nerves. I've been thinking, and I think because I'm so busy right now, I can't spend as much time with you as you'd like. Maybe you ought to think about other guys.

TAMARA   No, Paul. I don't want to do that. I know swimming means a lot to you. I don't mind waiting for you. You know I love you.

PAUL   Well, that's what bothers me. You don't do your own thing, but center your life around me. That makes me nervous. I'm not ready for that. I think we both need more space.

TAMARA (*getting upset*)   It's that Sybil girl on the swim team, isn't it? I told you she was a slut. She's been coming on to you, hasn't she? And because she's in her little wet bathing suit, you think about being with her, don't you?

PAUL   We don't have anything going on, if that's what you mean. But she is a nice girl, not a slut, and it gets on my nerves that you talk about her like that.

TAMARA   Yeah, sure. I've heard that before. Now you're sticking up for her. (*She rises and walks away, then calls back to him.*) You're not getting off the hook that easy, Paul. (*exits*)

PAUL and SYBIL are at a table in the branch library studying algebra. They laugh and joke, putting their heads together over the problems. TAMARA approaches outside the doors to return her library book, sees them, then turns away with her fists clenched.

TAMARA   That slut! I knew it. (*YOLANDA and ANDY are cruising by. They see her and stop.*)

YOLANDA   Hey, girl, what's up? I didn't know you hung out at the library.

TAMARA   I don't! But some sluts do!

ANDY   She sounds upset. Ask her if she wants a ride.

YOLANDA   It's dark out here. You want a ride?

TAMARA   No. I got business.

YOLANDA   In the dark? Come on, we were just going to go grab something to eat. You hungry?

TAMARA   No. I'm sick to my stomach.

ANDY   Tell her that's okay. I don't want anybody being sick in my car.

YOLANDA   Okay. See you tomorrow, then. (*YOLANDA and ANDY exit.*)

TAMARA goes around the side of the library, sits down in the shadows next to the building, and waits. An hour later, PAUL and SYBIL come out, talk a few minutes in the front of the entrance, then go opposite ways down the sidewalk. TAMARA begins to follow SYBIL.

SYBIL (*Hearing someone walking behind her, she turns, sees TAMARA, and stops.*)   Is that you, Tamara? What are you doing here?

TAMARA   Just got some business to take care of, slut!

SYBIL   Hey, what's the matter? I haven't done anything to you.

TAMARA   Sluts wouldn't get it anyway, so I'll show you. (*She grabs SYBIL by the hair and yanks her around. SYBIL grabs TAMARA'S arms and struggles. The two end up down on the sidewalk. TAMARA, still holding SYBIL'S hair, begins to bang her head up and down. Finally, TAMARA rakes SYBIL across the face with her long nails, leaving oozing gashes. TAMARA gives SYBIL a final kick in the stomach, then turns to leave.*) How's that, slut! So find your own boyfriend. People don't take stuff away from me!

SYBIL misses school and swim practice the next day. PAUL calls her to see what's the matter.

PAUL (*on the phone*)   Sybil! Where you been?

SYBIL   Paul? Oh, hi. I got bruised up a little.

PAUL   Oh, no. What happened? The swim meet's tomorrow. I hope you'll be able to make it. What happened?

SYBIL   I hate to tell you this, but we better cool it. Your girlfriend saw us in the library and decided to teach me a lesson, I guess. She waited for me after I left you last night and jumped me. My mom is so bent out of shape about this that she wants to put me in private school.

PAUL   Oh, my God. I'm so sorry. I did tell her I needed more space and that she should see other guys, but she didn't think much of the idea. But you can't quit. You're doing so great on the swim team.

SYBIL   Well, rough me up isn't all she did. She left some awful messages on the answering machine. And one of them was that she had some friends who were going to help her get justice. And that if I told anybody, I'd really be sorry. That I could really get hurt.

PAUL   She did that? Oh, my gosh. Maybe if I talked to her some more.

SYBIL   Thanks, but that just doesn't cut it. I'm not a fighter. I don't know what I'm going to do.

Discussion

1. Do you think Paul needs to be with Tamara as much as Tamara thinks she needs to be with Paul? What is the difference?
2. Tamara apparently hopes that by beating up Sybil she can keep Paul as her boyfriend. Is that likely to work? Can you *make* someone love you?
3. What consequences should Tamara face for her assault on Sybil?
4. What legal recourse does Sybil have against Tamara?
5. What should Sybil do about Tamara's threat for further harm if she told anyone?
6. Was Paul fair to Tamara when he broke up with her?
7. If you were in Sybil's shoes, what would you do?

Skit 39

I Got a Right to a Little Something

CHARACTERS
JEANNIE, HALLIE, TROY, MARVIN

JEANNIE, HALLIE, and TROY are at a party at MARVIN's house. In addition to alcohol, MARVIN is sharing some methamphetamine.

HALLIE (*on couch*)   So, Jeannie. Have you found out yet?

JEANNIE (*taking a swallow of beer*)   Oh, yeah. I am. The home pregnancy test came up positive, at least. But it's that jerk's fault.

HALLIE   You mean Troy? Why is it his fault?

JEANNIE   Because he was in a big hurry and didn't want to use anything. (*pause*) But I can't really blame him, I guess. I was pretty out of it.

HALLIE   Doing what?

JEANNIE   He had some potent pot, but I was already a little tipsy. So, you know, stuff happens.

HALLIE   Kinda like you are now? But you haven't used any meth tonight, have you?

JEANNIE   No, but I will if I get too depressed.

HALLIE   Does Troy know about the baby?

JEANNIE   No. I'm going to have to tell him when I know for sure, though. But until I see the doctor, the lid's off. (*She drinks more beer.*) But he probably won't care. He's cool. Especially after smokin' a little good stuff.

HALLIE   I thought it wasn't good for a baby to have a mother use stuff while she was pregnant. I don't mean to get in your business, but haven't you heard that?

JEANNIE   Yes, of course I've heard that. And you *are* nagging again, but you know my cousin from Los Angeles, she smoked blunts all during her pregnancy, and her baby came out with all its fingers and toes, so it's no big deal.

HALLIE   That's not what I hear. In health class, we studied fetal alcohol syndrome, where just a tiny bit of alcohol sometimes can harm a developing baby. And drugs can do all kinds of damage.

JEANNIE   Oh, please. I've got rights, too. If I really am pregnant, I'm going to be under a lot of stress. I've got a right to a little something to make me feel better. And if I feel good, the baby will feel good too. That seems like being kind, if you ask me.

TROY (*approaching*)   You guys look too serious. Come on, let's party. (*Grabs JEANNIE's hand and pulls her up.*) You're gonna get fat drinking all that beer. (*to HALLIE*) And you better check on Marvin. He's wigging. (*HALLIE goes to corner where MARVIN is sitting on the floor.*)

JEANNIE   Man, everybody's preaching at me tonight. But that's okay. It just means you care, right?

TROY   Yeah, I care. But don't count on me if you get fat.

JEANNIE   So, let's dance. I need the exercise. (*They dance a while until JEANNIE begins to feel nauseous. She turns pale and sweaty.*) Troy, I better sit down. I don't feel so good. I think the chips I ate didn't agree with me. (*She heads for the couch. He follows and plops down beside her.*)

TROY   Now what's the matter? You were sick yesterday, too. You're no fun. Rest a while and I'll check on you in a little while. (*He goes to see what MARVIN's doing in the corner.*) What're you doing down here, Marvin? What the heck's wrong with everybody tonight?

MARVIN Nothing, man. Just leave me alone, will you? Everybody's always in my face.

HALLIE (*to TROY*) He's been up for three days straight. He needs to crash. And he's not himself. I hate it when he gets all paranoid like this.

MARVIN (*to HALLIE*) You too? Just leave me alone, will you? Man, I have you guys over to my place, I give you top grade meth, and you won't leave me alone. Why don't you just take what's left and beat it? (*to TROY*) And your girlfriend, Jeannie. She's a drag. Give her some too. Then just leave, okay?

HALLIE (*to Troy*) We better go, Troy. I'm in the best shape to drive. Go get Jeannie, will you? (*She steps to table and scoops up the remaining crystals of meth, to herself.*) Oh, well. He said to help ourselves to it. I better brighten myself up a little if I'm going to drive. (*She snorts a line, then rubs her nose and approaches the others.*)

JEANNIE Man, I feel like I'm floating down a sewer. Any of that stuff left? I really am dragging.

TROY Yeah, sure. Marvin said to take it all. Give her some, Hallie. I saw you scoop it all off the table.

HALLIE I'm not really sure she should have any.

JEANNIE Come on, Hallie. Don't let me suffer like this. Come on. It won't hurt anything.

Discussion

1. Under what circumstances did Jeannie become pregnant?
2. Is there evidence that Jeannie and Troy have a strong, committed relationship? Explain.
3. How do you think a baby would feel about being conceived under such circumstances?
4. Is Jeannie ready for the responsibilities of parenthood? Explain.
5. From what you have seen so far, how has substance abuse affected each one of these kids?
6. How could they have fun at a party without substance abuse?
7. If Jeannie continues to use various drugs while she is pregnant, how could her baby be affected?
8. If Jeannie was your friend and you knew she was doing drugs while pregnant, what would you do?

Why Didn't You Tell Me You Had Something?

CHARACTERS
NEIL, CANDACE, GRACE, LARRY, NURSE

LARRY is in the NURSE's office.

LARRY (*He looks around to see if anyone can hear.*)   Um, I have this problem. It's kind of embarrassing. You won't tell anyone, will you?

NURSE   No, Larry. Nurses are like doctors or counselors. We keep the confidences of our patients, unless we feel someone is in mortal danger. Then the law requires us to report it so that lives can be saved. With certain diseases, though, we try to get the name of anyone else who might be infected so that they can be treated too. But it's all to protect people from sickness and save lives. So, do you still want to talk to me? I hope so. I'm here to help.

LARRY (*Clears his throat.*)   Well, I, um, have this burning when I pee. And stuff comes out of the end of my, you know, penis. This has never happened to me before.

NURSE   It's all right. We see young people in here often with similar problems. You did the right thing coming in. What you have sounds to me like a sexually transmitted infection. Have you been to your own doctor or a health clinic yet?

LARRY   Oh my gosh. I knew that girl Candace was trash. She sleeps with everyone.

NURSE   Larry, I can understand your being upset, but just because someone has contracted a sexually transmitted infection doesn't mean they're trash. In fact, chlamydia, which may be what you have, is as common as a cold among teens in this area.

LARRY (*bitterly*)   Boy, that really makes me feel better. But I gotta get rid of it. It's been like this for a while now. I thought it would just go away, but it hasn't. What do I do about it?

NURSE   No, it won't go away by itself. Sexually transmitted infections never go away by themselves. You asked what to do about it. Well, in this state, you can be treated for sexually transmitted infections without the authorities having to notify your parents. My job in this school is to educate and advise. I will refer you to the public health department, though. (*She hands him a card.*) You need to get down there as quickly as you can. They'll test you and diagnose just what infection or infections you may have, then treat you right away. The goal is to keep you and everyone you come in contact with healthy.

LARRY   You said "infections," with an "s." You mean I could have more than one?

NURSE   Yes, often these diseases travel in clusters. Someone can have one disease, give it to someone else with another disease, they infect each other, then the two of them can both give their two diseases to someone else, who may have a different disease, and so on.

LARRY   Now you're giving me the creeps.

NURSE   Better to find out now so you can get treated, and then you can be careful not to get infected again, or infect anyone else.

LARRY   Uh-oh. I hope I didn't infect my girlfriend. She'd kill me. She doesn't have to find out about this, does she? She doesn't know about that trash Candace.

NURSE   Well, they'll both have to be tested and treated.

LARRY   Man, I'm in big trouble.

NURSE   It has to be dealt with. Shall I call the health department for an appointment for you right now?

LARRY   I guess so.

LARRY calls CANDACE from a phone booth.

CANDACE   Hello?

LARRY   Hey, guess what I just found out?

CANDACE   Who is this? Is that you, Larry?

LARRY   You better know it is. You caused me a lot of trouble.

CANDACE   What are you talking about? Calm down.

LARRY   Well, I just visited the nurse. She thinks I have a sexually transmitted infection. Why didn't you tell me you had something?

CANDACE   Oh, sure. You get a disease, and you think you got it from me. Thanks a lot. You aren't exactly Mr. Clean yourself, you know. How do I know you didn't give me something? You've got a lot of nerve.

LARRY   Well, it's too late now, but I sure learned it's never smart to skip using a condom.

CANDACE   You make me sick. I better get checked to see if you gave me something. But you better be sure to let Grace know you're spreading disease. (*She hangs up.*)

After having visited the health department, LARRY approaches his friend NEIL who is seated at a lunch table with CANDACE and GRACE, his new girlfriend.

LARRY   Hi, everybody. Hey, Neil, can I talk to you a second? (*NEIL and LARRY step away from the table.*)

CANDACE (*calling after them*)   Don't let him give you any cooties.

NEIL   What's up?

LARRY   You been feeling okay lately?

NEIL   Yeah, sure. Why?

LARRY   Well, you know I was with Candace a few weeks ago. But we're not seeing each other now. Are you, you know, getting it on with her?

NEIL   And how is that any of your business?

LARRY   Well, I wish it wasn't, but I got a disease from her. I had to go to the health department and get treatment. I figure she gave it to me. So I thought I'd better warn you.

NEIL   No kidding? So you slept with her?

LARRY   Well, we didn't exactly sleep, if you know what I mean.

NEIL   How do you know Candace gave it to you? You did use protection, didn't you?

LARRY   Heck, no. I figured that was her problem. But I didn't know she was dirty.

NEIL   Blast it, Larry. She's not dirty. I haven't gotten anything from her. Maybe you got it someplace else. You been doing it with Grace?

LARRY (*clenching his fists*)   That sucks, man! How dare you suggest that Grace is sleeping around?

NEIL   Well, if you do the same thing, why can't she? Mellow out, man. Don't just blame it on the girl.

LARRY (*backing away*)   Okay. Okay. Forget it. Don't say I didn't warn you. But if you get a call from the health department, you'll know what's up. I had to tell them who I was with. They called it my "contacts." They'll call her, and if she has it, you could have gotten it from her, so they'll call you too.

NEIL   Hey, maybe you better grow up. A gentleman doesn't sleep around, and he doesn't blame the girl if something goes wrong. So how many people have *you* spread it to?

LARRY   Hey, I was just trying to help you out. Just drop it, okay? (*They return to the lunch table.*) Come on, Grace. This place gets on my nerves. (*She rises and they go into the cafeteria and sit down.*)

GRACE   What's the matter?

LARRY   Neil thinks he's some kind of a father or something. I hate when he tries to tell me what to do.

GRACE   About what?

LARRY   About who I hang out with.

GRACE   Was he talking about me?

LARRY   Yeah, but about Candace, too. You know I was with her before we got together.

GRACE   Yeah. I knew that. So?

LARRY   Well, she gave me a disease. Chlamydia. It's contagious. I might have given it to you. The health department says it won't go away by itself. I'm so sorry.

GRACE   I thought that's what you were upset about. Yeah, they called me yesterday. I've already been down there and started treatment. It's no big deal. Everyone gets stuff these days.

LARRY   But you told me it was your first time.

GRACE   Yeah, it was. With you. (*pause*) What are you staring at me for? Hey, this isn't the 1890s. Girls like to have a good time too. But I thought they'd be calling you. I gave them your name as one of my contacts.

LARRY   You lied to me. I thought you were a virgin.

GRACE   You know, I wish I still was. But I can't get it back. One other thing, though. The health department also tested me for HIV. People who have other sexually transmitted infections are at a bigger risk for becoming infected with HIV.

LARRY (*Turns pale.*)   What are you saying?

GRACE   Because it shows they don't use protection, and the invasion of another disease like chlamydia makes little breaks in the tissues that can let HIV in easier. You ought to be tested too.

LARRY   Do I ever feel like a jerk. And I thought I was such a stud.

GRACE   Yeah. Knowing all this makes you grow up fast, huh?

LARRY   For sure. But the people on TV never seem to get anything. I wonder how come.

Discussion

1. The young people in this story are sexually active. What do you think influenced them that it's okay to have casual sex?
2. What problem do you see with Larry blaming the girls he's had sex with for giving him a sexually transmitted disease?
3. What physical problems can occur from having untreated sexually transmitted infections?
4. If you were a counselor working with Larry, how would you try to help him protect himself from sexually transmitted disease in the future?
5. How would you try to help him with his attitudes toward young women?
6. What is the best way to protect yourself from getting any sexually transmitted infection?
7. Do you think practicing sexual abstinence would help or hurt the developing of quality relationships among these young people? Explain.